Choose Your Own Story

The Minecraft Zombie Adventure

John Diary

For Sarah.

I didn't know you when I wrote this, but somehow it was always for you.

Hey!

It's me, John Diary, the author. Before you get started, I wanted to tell you something very important.

This book is no normal book! In this book, you, not the author, get to decide what happens next. Start reading it like normal but at the end of each section you will get more or more choices of what you can do next. Choose what you want to do next and then flip to that page.

DON'T just flip through the pages of the book, because that will ruin the surprise! And also it won't make any sense!

There are twenty-six different endings in this book and three "happy" endings. Once you get to one ending, go back and start reading again. There are so many stories in this one book!

Happy reading,

John

John Diary

You wake up, and stretch your arms.

"EaaaaaaaUgghhhhh", you say. What? That's weird. Also your hands are stuck up in front of your face as if you were doing a Frankenstein impression. You can tell this is going to be one of those days.

You try again. "RaArrrrrrrrgh", you hear yourself say. Wow, you must have a cold, because you sound like your dad. Your dad when he wakes up in the middle of the night.

And your hands, by the way, are still sticking right out in front of you, they won't go any higher. You've never liked mornings. This morning is not changing that.

You sit up on the bed and look around. Your eyes must be blurry, because everything looks kind of blocky and pixelated. It's probably time to start the day.

If you want to get up and go to the bathroom, *turn to page 3*.

If you want to roll over and try to get back to sleep, *turn to page 5*.

Nothing's going to stop you! Rotney the Ruthless! You charge headlong into the player, your jaw wide open. It freaks you out a little bit to think about eating someone, but you're a zombie now, this is what you do. It kind of feels natural.

You bite him right in the back! It tastes weird, like metal and steak the way your grandpa makes it, all bloody and red. But then another taste comes into your mouth… pizza! Like fresh from the oven, pepperoni stacked, delicious cheesy pizza. This changes everything! No wonder zombies are always trying to eat people, they're freaking delicious!

The player swung their sword just as you went into bite, but it looks like they missed. Fibula though, who is now firing from right beside the player, had no chance to miss. FTHWANG! This player was starting to look like a porcupine. And not the kind that can run fast. The kind that your cousin has as a pet. And you don't understand why, because it does nothing but be a big ball of spikes! Worst. Pet. Ever.

The player backs up a little, he seems worried. You guys are awesome at being mobs!

If you want to let the player run away, *turn to page 46.*

If you want to go in for more delicious pizza flesh, *turn to page 8.*

You head to the bathroom, rubbing your eyes. You look in the mirror and are shocked by what you see. What... The... Nether?!

There's a gross, pixely, green face staring back at you. You recognize this, from your favourite game, Minecraft! You're a Minecraft zombie! What?! How did this happen?!

You remember that you fell asleep playing Minecraft last night. Your head sank right into your keyboard, spamming the chat with all sorts of crazy letters. Everybody else on the server must not have been happy. And you just fell asleep right there!

You must be dreaming! You try to pinch yourself, to wake up, but wait! You don't have fingers. Your hand is just a big green block. You can't pinch and just end up punching yourself. Ouch!

"GerBraaaaaaagh!" you say. But you still don't wake up.

You hear some clattering of wood or something outside the bathroom.

If you want to go check out the sound, *turn to page 30.*

If you want to try to wake yourself up using other methods, *turn to page 10.*

Stealth is key right here, there's no good in calling out and blowing your cover. You make a run for it now, you've got to reach the player first before he gets to your bossy skeleton friend or the jig is up! You burst forward, giving your legs all you've got. Back home, you won the track and field meet last year. Well, maybe not won, but you did pretty dang good. At least better than Jason in gym class who would not shut up about how fast he was.

You pretend that Jason is running beside you and give it the same burst of speed! You look down at your legs: they're still moving back and forth slowly like the stupid rectangles they are. How have you not learned this by now! Zombie legs are slow!

Oh no! If you can't get to the player fast because your legs move as fast as syrup that your mom accidentally put in the freezer, that means...

You look up. The player, shining in his blue armor has gotten right up behind Fibula. "Turn around!" you scream, but its too late. SHNICK SHNICK, the sword slices into the skeleton twice and a stack of bones pops into the air and falls a couple blocks away from the player. Fibula is gone.

But the player doesn't go to pick it up. Instead, he turns around to look at you. You really shouldn't have called out. Now you've got to run away! You turn around, running back for the hill. But, you guessed it, you're slow, the player's fast. From behind you, you hear SHNICK! That's all it takes.

The world flashes black. You die.

THE END

Don't worry though, you can always go back to see what would have happened if you'd tried something else. That's why this book is so special.

This day isn't turning out so well, maybe you can just skip it. You try to snuggle into your bed, pulling the covers up, but the bed feels weird. Maybe there's something hard in the bed, like a rock. Very hard, and very big. Maybe there's a boulder in your bed. What's going on?!

You really can't get comfortable. This bed is doing a terrible job of being a bed. Okay, that's it! You jump up and look at this stupid bed. It's not your bed, its wooden and blocky with red blankets and white sheets.

Oh no! That looks familiar. That's a Minecraft bed! You look at your hands, they are weird green cubes. You're in Minecraft! And judging by the colour of your skin, you're probably a zombie!

You've always kind of wanted to get to live in the world of Minecraft, there are so many possibilities! But, who wants to be a zombie? All you get to do is moan, bump into walls and turn into a toasty campfire when the sun comes up.

Maybe this is a dream?

If you want to go to the bathroom and look at yourself, *turn to page 3*.

If you want to try to wake yourself up, *turn to page 10*.

So, its pretty obvious that there are no cute girls in this room. This was kind of a silly plan, wasn't it. Well, don't feel too bad, zombies aren't very smart.

You find some lipstick in the cabinet in the bathroom. You put it on the rotting green flesh of your hand, trying to make some lips.

Examining your handiwork, you think, "That's pretty cute. For some rotting green hand lips, anyways."

You pucker up and go into kiss the hand. You try to say, "Amanda, you look lovely today." But it comes out as "BreAARGhhhhuuuuuuuuh." Then you close your eyes, this is the big moment, and kiss your hand.

Just then, you hear from the doorway "Ummmmm… what are you DOING?!"

Oh god, this is embarrassing. This HAS to be a dream, like those ones where you show up to school in nothing but your Spiderman underwear.

You turn around and see a Skeleton watching you from the doorway. Looking at you in shock, his jaw drops. But actually, his jaw drops on the floor. He quickly picks it up and clicks it back in. This gives you time to wipe the lipstick off your hand and straighten up.

"Uh, nothing," you say. I mean you actually say, "GreaaaaaaaghSPLUTZ." But the Skeleton seems to understand.

"C'mon, Mr. Hand-Kisser, we've got some scaring to do. Let's go!" and he rattles out of the room.

If you want to follow the skeleton, *turn to page 31*.

If you want to ignore him, *turn to page 19*.

You knock your foot against his and walk back down the hill with him. He's kind of a good guy after all, your plan to try to blow him up was a bit cruel. That player can just be left alone. Suddenly the urge to go after the player doesn't feel as strong. You're kind of happy being here with Fibula and T-Dawg. And even Mrs. Cube.

Fibula speaks up "Hey guys, I think we did a good job for tonight. Let's just head home."

You remember that you had another option. "Wait, Fibula do you know where we might be able to find an Enderman? Are there any in the area?"

"Uh, yeah, probably," the skeleton responds, "but it's getting early Rotney, the sun will be up in not so long. Maybe we just head back. Why are you so bothered anyways?"

Why WERE you so bothered about it? After all this, getting to know these people it was all seeming a little silly. Or maybe it was just the zombie brain slowly overwhelming your own. Your memories start slipping away and you move your tiny zombie legs as fast as you can to catch up with the rest of the group.

Fibula is telling the others about your daring moves against the player earlier! You were a hero and saved him. The others ooo and aww as they hear about your vicious bites and quick thinking. T-Dawg looks at you admirably.

You get back to the cave that you and Fibula seem to call home and you snuggle into bed for the day. Fibula appears at the door of you room. "Good work out there."

"Thanks," you say.

You fall asleep and the next night you get up and go scaring again.

And you fall asleep and do the same thing the next night. And the night after.

You're a Minecraft zombie now and it's not so bad after all.

THE END

Grarrr! You're a zombie now! And nothing will stop you! Players will pay! You go in for another bite!

This player has had enough of you, he jumps and dashes up the cliffside.

Dang, you just missed him with your bite. You try following him up the cliff but, you know, zombie legs. Like a seahorse at a horse race.

You watch the player duck into the little tunnel he came in and block it up with two cubes of cobblestone. He's gotten away, for now. The scent of his tasty pizza flesh still wafts around your mouth. Mmmmmm.

Fibula is delighted, he slaps you on the back, hopping up a storm. "Thank you Rotney, thank you! You saved my life, you know? How will I ever thank you?"

You swing your zombie leg a little, you don't know what to say. You were just doing what seemed right.

"And even better," Fibula cries, "We scared away a player! Oh those guys in the chunk over are going to have to stop making fun of us now. That wasn't no nube! That was a veteran. Diamond armor Rotney!" Fibula gets really up in your face. "DIAMOND ARMOR! We're getting a promotion!" He yells right into your face. Ugh, skeleton breath. It smells like... death, blank paper and sand.

"I'm happy to help," you say, "Just trying to do what's right. But that player he got away! I mean, shouldn't we go after him?"

Fibula is doing a tap dance. Oh wait, no, that's just a normal dance, his bones are the ones tapping. He looks up. "Go after him? What?"

"Go after him!" you insist!

"Uh, Rotney... did the witch doctor prescribe stupid pills? Because you're sure acting like it. He blocked up the path. There's no following him. I mean, I'm starting to forget that he was around at all, actually."

"We just go over and punch through the blocks..." you say and then you realize.

You're mobs. You can't punch blocks.

"You're really acting like a player right now, knock it off," says Fibula. "Come on, I'm going to go back to find the others, we've done more scaring than any other night already."

If you want to go back with Fibula, *turn to page 74*.

If you want to try to follow the player anyways, *turn to page 12*.

Okay, if this is a dream, you try to think about what will wake you up. Usually when you're having a dream you wake up just as you're about to kiss that really cute girl who sits beside you in class, or when you fall off something high, right before you hit the ground.

If you want to try the kissing method, *turn to page 6.*

If you want to try the falling method, *turn to page 18.*

You don't want to get down and dirty with that shiny blue sword. It's too dangerous. Anyways, the Skeleton seems to be taking care of himself. Look at him fire that bow. He's a real Robin Hood.

But the player is on top of Fibula right away, and Fibula's little hops are not doing enough to get him away from the player. "Uh oh," you realize, what were you thinking! There's no way that Fibula's going to get out of their alive.

You see the blue sword wing down into Fibula. Fibula is blasted away by the strength of the blow. He lets out another shot and it sticks into the player's armour.

Realizing what's about to happen you decide to start running! Let's get away from Evil Mr. Diamond Man! Behind you you hear the clatter of bones of Fibula falling to the ground. The poor sucker. Good thing you're running!

You look down at your legs. Oh Silverfish! Zombie legs! They're so slow, there's no way you're going to- You look behind you and there's the player with his inhuman helmeted face staring inquisitively at you.

"I JUST FOUND A ZOMBIE RUNNING AWAY, GUYS." The player says. It's weird when he talks, it seems to rattle the whole world and you see it pop up in text in the sky. That's how chat must look like from inside the game. You take his momentary distraction to keep running away. Sorry, crawling away.

"WHAT'S THAT ABOUT?" the world shakes.

"MUST BE A NEW UPDATE," it comes from a distance but still pops up in the sky.

"GUESS SO."

And with that, the player catches up and the diamond sword swings again.

You die.

THE END

You can always go back to see what would have happened if you'd tried something else!

Fibula starts walking back over the hill, but he stops when he sees you're not following.

You've climbed up the hill a little to look at the passageway that the player went through. The two blocks of cobblestone stick out sorely on the hillside, out of place. You know that the player is probably holed up in there. He likely has a mine in there and is just going to wait out the rest of the night. You've done it so many times before.

Maybe it's the new found undead bloodlust that you've discovered inside yourself, or maybe its just that you are intrigued to find another human on this server. If you had someway of communicating with him... He's in the outside world he might be able to get back to your family somehow to let them know you're stuck inside the game. Maybe he could just google for you how the heck to get out of a situation like this.

Your tummy grumbles. Okay, it's probably the undead bloodlust after all.

Why couldn't he just have put up a door? You could have handled a door!

"Geez, Rotney," says Fibula from down the hill. "Come on, let's go! There's no way through those things, there never have been. Only players can break blocks. That's their privilege, and they pay for it by being such insufferable, ugly, jerks. It's just their lot in life."

Fibula's right, it's true- NO! Fibula's wrong, you've been playing this game for a while, you're smarter than this! He's right that neither you nor can him can move those blocks, but there ARE mobs that can destroy blocks and some that can move them. creepers and Endermen. If you could just convince one of them to help you, you'd be able to go after this dumb player and either eat them or ask them for help, depending on what part of your brain you pay attention to: the human or the zombie.

Well, there's both T-Dawg and Teagan back where you came from that you could convince to help, but that would blow them up. They might not enjoy getting blown up, but then again: T-Dawg, who knows what's up with that guy.

On the other hand if you could get an Enderman to help, you could do this whole thing without getting anyone KABOOMified.

If you want to go get one of the creepers to help you, *turn to page 15.*

If you want to try to find an Enderman to help, *turn to page 60.*

You follow that familiar clicking noise up over the hill, watching Fibula jump and bob over the uneven terrain. On the other side of the hill the world opens up into grand canyons and towering mountains. The valley at the bottom of the hill cuts through them.

You can see for as far as the eye can reach. There's no weird cutoff of the surroundings like when you play the game. I guess things don't have to load when you're actually in the world of the game. There are some upsides to being stuck here. Man, this is the weirdest dream.

Fibula goes down into the valley, a steep cliff rises up beside him. You follow but you're lagging behind heavily. Zombie legs are like, the worst. It's like trying to ride a tricycle on the highway.

But maybe you're lucky being a little slower, because suddenly you see something bust through the cliff side behind Fibula. A diamond pickaxe carves through one then another block and then you can see it: a player, dressed head to toe in diamond armour. The weapon in his hand switches to a sword and he starts jumping down the slope. Fibula hasn't noticed at all and the player will be on him in a second.

All that diamond equipment is going to make it no issue to deal with Fibula. He's in trouble! Maybe two mobs would make it a fair fight, but its going to be dangerous anywhere near that diamond sword. You've got to make up your mind right now! Go!

If you want to run down the hill to try to save Fibula, *turn to page 24.*

If you want to quickly hide on the other side of the hill where the player can't see you, *turn to page 20.*

"Hey Fibula," you say, "Do you think T-Dawg is still back in the crater?"

"Yeah, probably, he hasn't got much in that head of his except dynamite."

You head back over the hill to the clearing where you started the scaring. Not very surprisingly, T-Dawg is stuck in the corner of a cliff just kind of bumping into things. A big jelly hangs out nearby him. You immediately stop in your tracks when you see the thing. Those guys always give you so much trouble, it sucks that every time you hit them they just get smaller, more plentiful, and harder to hit. It feels like when your twin little sisters are trying to touch all the stuff in your room. Except you're not allowed to whack them with a pickaxe.

Fibula looks back at you, and you smack yourself in the forehead. Right, zombie. We're all on the same team here, nothing to worry about.

Fibula asks, "Wait, what are we doing again?"

"You'll see," you smirk. You haven't got a plan yet, but you'll figure something out. "Hey T-Dawg! How's it going? Sweet cliffs you got here."

"Oh thanks man, yeah, these are some beauties right here. Really great for bumping into."

You nod. "Cool…"

"Oh, I should introduce you!" T-Dawg points to the Jelly squelching beside him with his tiny, adorable little leg. "This is Mrs. Cube. She was just telling me about how she almost got to absorb a player the other day. She got real up close, just wanting to keep the player safe inside her big jelly embrace. But as she touched him, he rudely died on her, right there. Exploded into a billion pieces and all of his items fell everywhere. How disappointing."

"So you just wanted to keep the player safe? You weren't trying to hurt him?" you ask the jelly.

It bops at you in silence for a second.

"She's shy," T-Dawg cuts in. You begin to wonder if the cube has ever said anything or if its just in T-Dawg's dynamite-filled mind.

"But," T-Dawg continues, "You're right. We never really want to hurt any players."

You look at Fibula sideways. What?

"I mean I know that Fibula always wants us to do our work and make sure we scare people, and I try to do my best, but, you know I've never really felt that way. I just think- players are so cool! They're all, 'Look I have hands and can use tools and I build stuff and when I talk it appears in letters in the sky.' I mean, they're basically… gods…" T-Dawg seems caught up in a dream, staring into space.

"So then why are you always trying to blow them up?" you ask.

"Blow them up, oh Mod no! I never want to do that. I really just want… a hug. You know? I want to touch them."

"But creepers are always blowing up…" you point out.

"Oh, well, we're not great at controlling our emotions. And whenever they get out of hand we are known to… make a scene. And the excitement of seeing a player is just too much for some of us!"

All of you, you think to yourself. But this totally changes the way you think about creepers. Did they really just want a hug this whole time? Okay, but back to the plan.

"Well, you're in luck," you tell T-Dawg, "there's a player hanging out in the valley on the other side of the hill, and he seemed pretty friendly really."

"What?" says Fibula, while T-Dawg explodes with excitement. Well, no, not 'explodes'. That was a bad choice of words, but he gets very excited.

"Oh my Mod! Really?! Thank you Rotney! Thank you! Come on Mrs. Cube, let's do this, this is finally my moment." T-Dawg hops up the hill while the cube just kind of stands there squelching.

You shoot a look at Fibula that says, shhhh, you'll see, as you follow after him.

16

When T-Dawg and you get to the other side he looks around disappointedly.

"Where's the player?"

"Oh shoot," you say, "I guess he must have wandered off. Wait! Do you see these two cubes in the cliffside?" You walk over to the two blocks with him.

"Cobblestone?!"

You wait for T-Dawg to make the connection. Nothing happens.

"Which means?" you prompt.

Nothing.

"The player might have gone through there…" you say.

"OOOOHhhhhh. You're smart Rotney," says T-Dawg, "But I guess he's gone now. Too bad."

"What that's it? Don't you want to get through here, and find him?"

You see Fibula watching you and shaking his skull.

"How are we going to do that Rotney?" T-Dawg asks, "I can't move blocks. Heck, I don't even have arms."

Hmm, you didn't really think this through.

T-Dawg looks at the cobblestone in front of him, and shrugs, as much as you can with no real shoulders. "Well, good try Rotney. Thanks for looking out for me. Leg bump!" He sticks out his little shrimpy leg.

If you want to give him a leg bump and go back, *turn to page 7.*

If you want to tease him about his legs, *turn to page 47.*

You notice there's a big cabinet in the bathroom. You could probably jump off of that. But how to get up there? Think Minecraft. You've got to jump on something that's one block high so you can jump on something that's two blocks high, so you can get on top of the three block high cabinet. Luckily, the toilet and the sink are lined up. Here goes!

Once you've jumped on the sink you check yourself out in the mirror: Your light blue shirt really brings out your sickly green skin.

You jump to the top of the cabinet and look down at the cobblestone floor of the bathroom. You take a deep breath and get ready to jump, this better be a dream or this is going to hurt.

You count yourself in 1. 2. 3. JUMP! But you don't, you're just standing there. You try again and still your legs are stuck to the top of the cabinet. It's like you can't, like you're not programmed to be able to jump. Programmed! That's it! You're a mob of course, and mobs can't willingly jump off such tall things. Dangit.

Just as you're thinking that, you hear a clattering at the door. There's a skeleton standing there looking up at you. "What are you doing NOW?!"

"Ummmmm," you say, "I thought I saw some brains up here." That seemed like a good excuse. Even though the words come out as a low moan, the skeleton still understands. You climb down from the cabinet, embarrassed.

"Great, well keep looking," says the skeleton, "If you had a couple more brains maybe you wouldn't do dumb stuff like this. Come on, we've got some scaring to do, we're already late!" And he clatters out of the room.

If you want to follow the skeleton, *turn to page 31.*

If you want to ignore him, *turn to page 23.*

You just stand in the room. Well, this is kind of boring. Do you want to do something?

If you want to follow the skeleton, *turn to page 31.*

If you want to try to wake yourself up by falling, *turn to page 18.*

If you want to just hang out, *turn to page 25.*

This is no time to be a hero, you quickly, or as quickly as your silly zombie legs can, jog back down the hill and duck where the player can't see you. That was a lot of diamond equipment down there and you are a zombie. A zombie! Let's just say that a zombie is to a diamond sword like a block of butter is to a hot butcher knife. One zombie is going to become two half zombies very quickly.

You hear the rattle of Fibula distantly over the hill. No bow firing yet, you guess that Fibula hasn't noticed yet. That means he's in trouble!

If you want to muster your courage and try to save him, *turn to page 24.*

If you want to go back and try another direction, *turn to page 39.*

You follow distantly behind Teagan towards the river. The landscape is truly beautiful here, it really shouldn't be any different than seeing the game on your computer, but everything just seemed much more majestic, kind of like nature in the real world.

Maybe you'd think that because everything was made out of cubes it wouldn't be as beautiful, but it was almost more exciting because it was so strange! As you watch the wide river flow distantly in front of you, majestic, powerful, moving fast, for a second you let yourself just be super excited about being in Minecraft! This is kind of a dream come true, it's your favorite game after all. It was like you were wearing some of those futuristic virtual reality goggles, everything around you was a game.

Your brain nags you that you should be worried, you do seem to be trapped in a game as a very squishy mod that could easily get poked to death. What happens if you die as a zombie? Do you- wake up? Or do you… It's too scary to think about. You go back to looking at the river, there are squid swimming around in it. You let out a little "Wow…" Well, actually, it's more like "Wablaaaaaaaugh", but you get the idea.

Suddenly you realize you're not alone. Teagan has stopped and is watching you.

"You're a weird one, Rotney," she says. And if you're not mistaken, you think that creeper just smiled at you. You didn't think that that animation existed in the game.

You are suddenly embarrassed. You know that really Teagan is just a bunch of bits and bytes, just a creeper on a server. But something about the way she said "you're a weird one", reminds you of that girl who sits beside you in class. She says the same thing when you cut a slit in your eraser and make it a little dude with a huge mouth.

You turn away uneasily, "Uh, I was just thinking about something else." This was not a good cover. "Something crazy, like a scarf for a giraffe." That's worse.

She laughs and her laugh sounds very much like the hiss of an exploding creeper. It gives you half a heart attack! You jump away.

"Woah, Are you okay?!" she asks.

"Oh, yup, fine." You didn't need that half of your heart anyways. "Just thinking about that giraffe scarf again."

You start walking towards the river and she waddles behind you.

"I think you're right, you know?" she says after a second.

"Hmm?" you say.

"About the river. I think you're right. It is 'wow'," she says. "It's beautiful. But, I never really think any of the others really feel that way."

Who knew creepers could be so reflective? They're not all explosions and totally freaking your face off.

"Rotney, you're sooooo sensitive." Now, she's making fun of you.

"Uh, aren't we supposed to be like scaring players or something?" you say, trying to change the subject.

"Yeah, I guess so." She seems pleased with herself. "Where do you want to go? I'm thinking over near that big tree over there? Or we could try to cross the river?"

If you want to go over to the large tree, *turn to page 75.*

If you want to cross the river, *turn to page 66.*

You just stand in the room. Well, this is kind of boring. Do you want to do something?

If you want to follow the skeleton, *turn to page 31.*

If you want to try to wake yourself up by kissing something, *turn to page 6.*

If you want to just hang out, *turn to page 25.*

Fibula is your only friend out here right now, you have to save him!

You head off as fast as your mostly dead zombie legs will take you. Being a zombie right now is a real bummer.

Despite your best efforts, the player is almost on top of Fibula and you're still pretty far away. What are you going to do?!

If you want to call out to Fibula and warn him, *turn to page 32.*

If you want to keep running up behind the player, *turn to page 4.*

John Diary

You're just standing in a bathroom. You watch a bug fly around and land on the toilet. Weird, you don't see bugs in Minecraft when you play the game.

You try to twiddle your thumbs, but you don't have thumbs.

If you want to finally follow the skeleton, *turn to page 31*.

If you want to just stay in the bathroom, *turn to page 27*.

You arrive back in the plains where you started the scaring with T and T and Fibula. The moon hangs heavy in the sky, the darkness has settled on the land, but you can see through it as if it were the middle of the day. Zombie legs might be terrible but zombie eyes have their upside.

You see T-Dawg in the corner still bumping into the sides of a cliff, he's really not very smart. A big jelly sits nearby him, plopping along lazily. Those things usually give you the creeps when you're playing, but now, you realize, they can't do anything to you. The night is safe, except for those no-good players.

Fibula wanders over to go talk to T-Dawg. Out of the corner of your eye you see him trying to convince the creeper to maybe try walking in a different direction. T-Dawg is going to have none of it though. 'Good for him', you think, 'at least that dumb creeper knows what he wants.'

To your left you see the hills that Fibula went over. In front of you is the way to the river. And on the right is the big forest. Its trees loom over you uneasily. Something calls to you from the forest.

If you want to go to the river, *turn to page 21.*

If you want to go to the woods, *turn to page 70.*

You start counting zombie sheep. There really isn't a lot to do in a bathroom. Especially when you're a zombie, in a video game. Maybe a shower is a good idea? While you're killing time at least.

If you want to go check out whatever that skeleton was talking about, *turn to page 31.*

If you want to take a shower, *turn to page 28.*

You step into the shower and turn on the faucet, a bright glowing block of orange materializes under the tap. OH SHEEP!

That's lava! You take a step back, but the lava is already filling the room, blocking the door. Who puts a lava shower in a house?! You don't have much time to think about it because the lava catches you on fire. The world pulses bright orange for a second before everything goes black. You die.

THE END

You follow the skeleton out into the night. The Minecraft landscape, it's a forest biome, is pitch black but you don't have any problem seeing, it's like your eyes were made for this. You wish your eyes were always like this, it would make reading books after bedtime SO much easier.

As you walk, the skeleton goes on and on about scaring.

"So you see we've really been slacking off on our area recently, we've been in the lead for most players on our section night after night." He's hopping fast and you are trying to keep up.

"Oh, well… that's good." you say, you weren't really listening. Come on listen up, do you have gravel in your ears?

"NO, no, it's BAD! We're supposed to be keeping them away. The guys on the section over are saying that we even let a noob survive his first night without making a dirt house. It's not true, obviously, but that looks bad for us. We need to shape up." He seems hopping mad. Heh, hopping, you giggle at yourself.

"Not funny. Oh good, here's T-Dawg." he points with his bony arm. T-Dawg appears to be the name of the creeper wandering towards you. Instinctively you back away!

"Woah, calm down there, bucko. You're acting like a real player right now." The skeleton says "player" like it was a bad word.

"Okay remember," the skeleton whispers, "Don't mention T's stumpy little legs, it makes him mad!"

T-Dawg walks up and hisses at you guys. "Hey you guys! LEG BUMP!" he shouts, putting one of his truly tiny little legs out for you to bump.

If you want to do a leg bump, *turn to page 43*.

If you want to tease T-Dawg about his tiny legs, *turn to page 33*.

You follow the rattling sound down the hallway. It grows louder as you reach the room at the end of the hallway. *Click clack, rattle tattle.* You cautiously peek your head through the door and see in the shadowy, light a skeleton, hopping in the middle of the room. He seems a little miffed.

"There you are! Come on, out the door, we're late for scaring." It clicks and rattles at you, but you understand the words anyways.

"Scaring?" you ask. Your voice comes out as if you had just been hit between the legs with a soccer ball, "BlughGRAAAARRblugh?" But he seems to know what you mean.

"Yeah man, what we do every night. Are you feeling okay? You seem more braindead than your normal braindead self. If that's possible."

You kind of stare at the skeleton blankly.

"You know? When we go out at night and just kind of wander around and freak out the players?" he asks condescendingly.

"Oh yeah!" you say, "Scaring, of course."

He shakes his head. "Zombies. Honestly, why do I even bother.

He grabs his bow and hops out the door into the night. "We've got a scare quota to keep up, get your blue-jeaned butt moving! If you don't, I'm firing this at YOU."

I guess you don't really have a choice here.

To head off to do some scaring, *turn to page 29.*

You follow the rattling sound down the hallway. It grows louder as you reach the room at the end of the hallway. *Click clack, rattle tattle.* You walk in and see the skeleton, hopping in the middle of the room, he seems a little miffed.

"There you are! Come on, out the door, we're late for scaring." It clicks and rattles at you, but you understand the words anyways.

"Scaring?" you ask.

"Yeah man, what we do every night. Are you feeling okay? You seem more braindead than your normal braindead self. If that's possible."

You kind of stare at the skeleton blankly.

"You know? When we go out at night and just kind of wander around and freak out the players?" he asks condescendingly.

"Oh yeah!" you say, "Scaring, of course."

He shakes his head. "Zombies. Honestly, why do I even bother."

He grabs his bow and hops out the door into the night. "We've got a scare quota to keep up, get your blue-jeaned butt moving! If you don't, I'm firing this at YOU."

I guess you don't really have a choice here.

To head off to do some scaring, *turn to page 29.*

You've got to warn that plucky little skeleton!

"FIBULA!" you yell, "Look out behind you!" but it comes out all "FLAAAAAARRRRRRGHbluck".

The player turns around quickly and looks at you. Then looks back at Fibula.

Fibula whips around and notices the player! He raises his bow, and takes a shot, it sticks right into the player's leg. This guy knows what he's doing!

You stop in your tracks now that the player is looking right at you, you know what a sword like that can do to a green-skinned little mob like you. You have first hand experience! And your mom said that all that Minecraft was a waste of time. Now it's saving your life!

Seeing you stop, the player starts running at Fibula, who tries to hop backwards while firing the bow a second time, he hits again. Seriously, this guy is good. You think back to all those times that you met that one frustratingly accurate skeleton while you were playing Minecraft. Maybe it was Fibula. This time though you're quite pleased at how accurate this skeleton is.

His eagle-like precision doesn't slow down the player though, who catches up to Fibula in a hurry.

If you want to try to bite the player, *turn to page 2.*

If you want to keep your distance, *turn to page 11.*

You look down at the little leg that he's holding out and say, "Oh my god, your leg's so small, I almost missed it entirely. I was like 'What leg?!'"

T-Dawg's beady little black eyes stare into you. The skeleton freezes in horror.

"Man, you should be a pirate," you continue, "you'd get discount peg legs."

A violent hiss starts coming from T-Dawg.

"You know? Because it would take so little wood."

The hissing gets louder. Uh oh. Well, you thought you were funny.

SHKABANG! What used to be you and the skeleton and T-Dawg is now just one big crater. You die.

THE END

You stop climbing up the ladder. "Uh," you say, "maybe this isn't such a good idea."

"What?!" says Teagan. "Come on, keep going!"

"No, go back!"

"How? You didn't tell me how to go back!"

"Walk backwards?"

"I'll fall off!"

"You won't!"

"Um, Rotney."

"What?"

"Rotney…" she's nodding behind you. You turn around, there's a very shocked looking player wearing a bronze helmet staring at you from up the ladder. Your zombie moans must have given you away.

"WOAH, YOU GUYS WON'T BELIEVE WHAT I'VE JUST FOUND," he says. The world rumbles and you see his words pop up in the air. "THERE'S A ZOMBIE AND CREEPIE JUST CLIMBING MY DANG LADDER!"

Suddenly his hand has a sword in it. Uh oh. He hits you once and you get pushed off the ladder. As you fall you hear an explosion go off above your head. Little trunks of tree and the belongings of the player fall through the air beside you then THWACK! You hit the ground and die.

THE END.

Don't worry though, you can always go back to see what would have happened if you'd tried something else. There are so many different endings you can find if you're clever enough. One of them even will take you to the sequel: Minecraft Zombie Adventure 2: Journey to the Ender.

"Uh, well, there is something," you say.

"Really?" she says with a smile.

"You promise not to laugh?" you ask.

"Promise. If I had a hand to put over my heart, I'd do it."

You build up your courage by taking in a long, slow breath. It doesn't do anything. Zombies don't breath, smarty-pants.

"Well you said you like me today, well I like you too. Today. I mean, I feel we didn't get a chance to know each other before today. There's just something about you."

She smiles a huge smile at you. And then the hissing starts.

"Give me a second," she says. She closes her eyes. And takes a deep breath.

The hissing is good news, you think. It means she is feeling something strong right now, is it happiness? It's good news as long as she doesn't blow you up.

The hissing stops.

"Well that's the best news I've ever heard," she says, opening her eyes. "Sorry about that, I get blowy-uppy when I get happy."

Yes!

"I mean, it's weird," she says, "you're a zombie, I'm a creeper. But you're not a normal zombie and I like to think I'm not a normal creeper. So maybe it makes sense."

If only she knew just how weird it was. But sometimes life is like that. I mean, you're already stuck in a video game, might as well make the best of it.

She gives you a quick kiss. It's… explosive, for lack of a better word.

"Come on," she says, "let's go back."

You talk her down the ladder, while she's nervous at first, she trusts you so it's easy to teach her how to climb down.

"Do you think T-Dawg will be okay with us?" you ask at the bottom of the ladder.

"Sure," Teagan says, "He loves you. Just don't make fun of his legs, okay?"

"Roger," you say.

As you walk back to the clearing where you started, she says, "If I had a hand, I'd hold yours."

Kind of gross, but kind of sweet. If you're going to be stuck in this weird blocky world, at least it can't get any better than this.

THE END.

Congratulations! You made it to the end. But, you can always go back to see what would have happened if you'd tried something else. There are so many different endings you can find if you're clever enough. One of them even will take you to the sequel: Minecraft Zombie Adventure 2: Journey to the Ender.

You climb down the ladder again. When you're halfway down, Teagan calls down to you from above. "Wait, Rotney how do I get down!?" She's standing at the top of the ladder looking down nervously. "You never taught me."

"Well," you say, "you just go to the ladder and walk backwards. That's it."

"What?!" she says. "I can't hear you!"

You've gotten to the bottom of the ladder at this point and apparently you're too far away for Teagan to hear you well. You shout up again.

"JUST WALK BACKWARDS!"

She gets up to the ladder and takes a couple hesitant steps backwards. Great! You take one step to the side of the ladder to get a better view. Just as she's about to come out of the trapdoor of the tree house she yells down to you again.

"Wait, Rotney! ROTNEY! If I keep walking backwards, aren't I just going to fall backwards off the ladder?!"

"No, no, you'll be fine." It occurs to you that maybe one of the most dangerous places to stand is under a panicky creeper on a ladder who doesn't know how to use a ladder. It's like standing beneath a pile of lit dynamite, precariously balanced on the edge of a ten story building, in a wind storm.

"WHAT?!"

It seems that creepers really have terrible hearing. 'To be fair, they don't have ears,' you think to yourself.

"YOU. WILL. BE. FINE," you yell back. "Walk backwards and whatever you do, don't walk sideways!"

"What?! What did you say? Walk sideways!?"

"No! No! No! No!" you shout. But it's too late.

She takes a side step off the ladder, towards you and starts plummeting towards the ground. Just your luck. She could have just as easily gone in the other direction, but no, of course not. Anyways, there's no time to think about how unlucky you are, you have to start running!

You move your zombie legs as fast as you can from the bright green screaming bomb falling towards you. You think it's the most speed you've ever gotten on these half dead limbs of yours. But still you're a zombie. It's not fast.

You hear a thud behind you, not far enough away. And then the whole world flashes white and you and Teagan turn into a crater beneath a treehouse. You die.

THE END.

Don't worry though, you can always go back to see what would have happened if you'd tried something else. There are so many different endings you can find if you're clever enough. One of them even will take you to the sequel: Minecraft Zombie Adventure 2: Journey to the Ender.

You turn your back on your friend and lope back down the hill.

You hear the sound of a bow firing and then the SHNICK of a sword. Fibula's bones clatter twice more and then with another final swipe of the sword there is silence. You don't linger for long. You can't, it might be dangerous.

'It was just a Minecraft skeleton," you tell yourself. 'Just a Minecraft skeleton.' It really shouldn't effect you. He wasn't real.

But then, you think, 'I'm just a Minecraft zombie. And I'm real. I think?' You really need to wake up from this crazy dream.

With that, you trek back down the hill. A couple times you think that you can hear the familiar rattle of Fibula's walk, and you look behind you. But, it's nothing. Just a hallucination. Just wishful thinking.

Now, turn to page 74.

That hiss can only mean one thing and you turn on your rotting heel and start moving as fast as you can. You know that you have zombie legs, and they're not fast, but they'll be faster than the tiny stubs that creepers have for legs. You'll be able to outrun her at the very least.

As you take a couple steps away, you hear Teagan break into tears.

"Wait, no, don't go! This is what always happens, everyone that I like, they're scared of me! I can't really like anyone! I don't blame you for running, I guess. But please, it doesn't have to be like this!" she starts running after you. The hiss gets even louder!

"No!" you cry, "Don't follow me! You're going to blow both of us up!"

"Don't run then! Stay with me!" she says.

You don't have a choice, it's bye-bye if you stick around. You keep running! But not fast enough.

When she sees you not stop, she lets go one giant wail of sadness. Then BOOM! You aren't far enough away. You die.

THE END

Of course it's worth it! Going back would be silly at this point anyways, does Teagan even know how to climb down a ladder?

You keep climbing up the ladder, nearing the bottom of the treehouse. You get to the trap door, take a deep breath. This is it. You pop through the floor and see a player, dressed in a bronze helmet, purple pants and a checkered shirt. He's standing near a lit furnace, smelting something.

The treehouse is just a platform on top of the tree, decked out with torches and totally surrounded by fences. It's a good size with a good view of the rest of the plane.

He must have heard the sound of your footsteps, because he turns around in a second. He stands there staring at you. You can only imagine that he's feeling pretty shocked right now, when's the last time you saw a zombie climb a ladder twenty blocks into the air?

"WHAT THE-" he says.

His hand suddenly has an iron sword in it. Here we go! It's go time. You feel a little scared fighting this guy, but I guess you have to start biting or otherwise you'll end up just a mostly useless pile of rotting flesh. If you lose, who knows what happens then?

Then, Teagan pops up through the floor and appears beside you.

The player takes a step and then stops in his tracks looking at Teagan.

"THIS IS THE WORST DAY EVER," he says. Apparently he's not a fan of a creeper just suddenly showing up in his cool tree house.

You brace yourself for his strike but instead he just turns around and hops up onto the top of one of the railings. He looks back for a second and then jumps!

You and Teagan rush over to the railing.

"He got away!" Teagan says, mournfully.

You both look down, over the railing, the drop is pretty far. At the bottom of it, you can see in the pale moonlight a pile of floating objects: a sword, axe, blocks of dirt, wood, a couple bars of gold. It doesn't look like the poor player made it.

"Oh," says Teagan. "He didn't really get away." This news doesn't seem to encourage her at all.

"I guess that was our goal, right? We did it?" you say. "You don't seem pleased."

"Yeah, no," she says, "it's great." But you don't believe her.

If you want to go down and loot all those sweet items the player dropped, *turn to page 37.*

If you want to ask Teagan what's wrong, *turn to page 82.*

You kick his little foot with your leg. He seems pleased.

"I've always liked you Rotney," he says.

Rotney! You have a name, I guess.

"Where's Teagan?" asks the skeleton.

"Ah, T? She's just coming over the hill." says T-Dawg.

You look up to see another creeper hopping over the top of the hill in front of you. Teagan and T-Dawg. T and T. TNT. Ahhhh, you get it now.

"Alright, now that we're all here," says the skeleton, "Our zone extends from the river in the north to the caves in the east so let's spread out and find some of those no-good players."

"You're the boss Fibula," Teagan says as she joins the huddle. The skeleton has a name too!

The other three spread out and start looking for players. Fibula, the skeleton, goes over the hill. Teagan heads to the river and T-Dawg just kind of bumps into some cliffs in a corner. He seems like a genius. What are you going to do?

If you want to go over the hill, *turn to page 14.*

If you want to go to the river, *turn to page 21.*

If you want to head off alone to the woods, *turn to page 70.*

You take a couple steps back and tell Fibula to get clear, you are going to try something crazy. You go to the edge of the plateau, take a deep breath, and stare directly at Portia, who is now just standing near the edge of the plateau looking out.

It only takes a couple seconds before she notices. Without having seen you she spins around and perfectly stares into your eyes. You realize that you don't like being looked at much either, at least not by Endermen.

She lets out a little scream and teleports directly in front of you.

"Don't Stare!" she shrieks. She shakes and swings at you. It's a terrifying sight.

You start to run down the hill and into the valley. You've never been fast, but this time you're in more trouble, because the creature chasing you has something you maybe didn't fully realize. The ability to teleport.

The minute you start to run, she's in front of you, shaking with rage.

You try to take a quick left and get around her, but there she is again, her eyes glowing red. You realize you've made a mistake, you try to turn around to apologize. But, before you have time to say a single thing, her face fills your vision, its mouth open, and her shriek fills your ears. The world is nothing but shrieking and fear. She strikes. You die.

THE END

You grab Teagan. "You have to calm down, or we're both done for."

She looks at you, her eyes full of fear.

"I'm not a player. I'm a zombie, remember? I'm just a zombie. I'm a zombie," you say.

The hiss grows a little quieter. You just keep repeating it. "I'm a zombie, just a dumb old zombie."

The hiss gets even quieter. Teagan says, "Just a dumb zombie. With a little bit of player in there somewhere."

Don't say that! But it's nothing to be worried about, because somehow, with that, the hiss stops. Teagan takes a deep breath.

"You okay?" you ask.

"Yep. For now. But you should probably go. I'm too dangerous. Especially around you."

She has a point, you guess. But as stupid as it is, you like her. This isn't fair, what do you do? Why can't you just get out of this dumb game?

If you want to leave Teagan, *turn to page 52*.

If you want to stay with Teagan, *turn to page 102*.

You relax a second. You've won, Fibula is safe, the player is going to get out of here. Run little player, run!

But, it looks like he doesn't really want to run away anyways. He stands there for a second and then seeing that you've stopped going after him, he dives back in sword swinging! Oh boy…

You shouldn't have given him a second to breathe. It's clear that you guys aren't a match for him.

"Run!" you yell at Fibula.

You go back in for another bite, but the player hits you with his sword first. You think you have one bite left in you, and you go for it, you have to give Fibula a chance to get away. Taking a split second to look back at him, you see Fibula is still there, dumb thing! Does he even have a brain?! Oh, probably not.

Whether it's his brave stand to protect his friend or just the way Mojang programmed mobs, Fibula is staying by your side to protect you. He fires another arrow into the player's chest. It slows the player down for a split second before he swings his sword and everything goes black.

You die.

THE END

You have an idea.

You look down at his leg he's sticking out for the bump. "Oh my Mod," you say, picking up his vocabulary, "why do you have a growth coming out the side of you body?"

"What?!" T-Dawg looks around frantically. "A growth?!"

You take a step back. "Yeah, a growth! It's right where your- oooohhhhhhh. Never mind."

"Never mind! What, where is it?" he's spinning around.

You take a step back.

"It's nothing."

You take another step back.

"What was it? I don't get it," T-Dawg complains.

You shuffle back a little further. "Oh, it was just, well… It was your leg. It was so small you know that I mistook it for a growth, which is super embarrassing."

The ominous hiss starts coming from T-Dawg. You start running away in earnest now. You shout back over your shoulder, "I mean it would be almost better if it was a growth. I think a big ugly weird growth would be better than having legs smaller than a Shih Tzu! Or one of those wiener dogs."

That's done it. You scramble to get far enough away as the hissing behind you gets louder and louder. Then KABLOWEY!

You look back to see a big chunk of the cliff, and T-Dawg, missing. Blocks sit everywhere, thrown from the explosion. And in the center of the cavity carved out of the cliff you see a little opening. There it is. A two block tall corridor opens up into the side of the mountain, that's where the player went.

You notice Fibula watching you, he seems disappointed, he's shaking that little skull of his again. He makes a little clicking sound with his jaw.

"That wasn't cool Rotney, T-Dawg was a good guy. I kind of liked his whole dumb thing. Why did you want to go after that player so bad anyways? He might be gone already. We don't hold grudges, remember, we just protect our territory. And we definitely don't blow up cool creepers just to have a chance to hunt down one single player."

You feel bad, but you go up to the entranceway and look inside.

"I'm not going with you," he says, "I don't know what's gotten into you. You can do this weird thing by yourself. Bye Rotney." He turns around and clatters up the hill.

If you want to enter the passageway by yourself, *turn to page 57*.

If you want to catch up with Fibula, *turn to page 51*.

"Uh, well," you say, "there is something."

"Really, what?" she asks.

"This is going to sound crazy, seriously. Like I'm going to sound absolutely nuts."

"Okay, I can deal. I just told you that I want to hug your worst enemy in the world. I think we're past the point of crazy."

"Yeah, but this is next level crazy," you insist. "If I'm going to tell you I need you to promise that you're not going to think I'm crazy. Or really tell anyone. Okay?"

"Okay. I promise." You think you can trust her.

You take a deep breath. Here goes. "So, I'm not a zombie. I mean, I look like a zombie and I have a zombie's body, but inside, I'm not Rotney."

"Wow, you really aren't yourself today," she says. It's funny, but you can tell she's a little concerned.

"This morning I woke up inside this zombie body. But this is not what my normal life is like. Does that make sense?"

"I guess. Maybe?" she says.

'I mean, how could it, she's just a couple of bytes,' you think.

"So, what are you normally then?" she asks.

"This is where it gets hard to explain. I'm a, well, a person?"

She looks at you blankly, but that might be normal creeper face.

"Okay, what if I told you that players were not exactly what they looked like, but they're actually being controlled by creatures in a different world. We use computers, which are like red stone machines, but really, really complex, and shrunk much smaller and we control characters in this world, which show up to you as players."

"Okay, this seriously sounds absolutely crazy," Teagan says. "But, somehow I believe it. Like players do seem a little like they're from a different world."

"Yeah! Well, I'm really one of those creatures from a different world, and I often play- well, control one of the players in this world, like I do it all the time. And I fell asleep last night while controlling a player and when I woke up this morning, I was- me." You point to yourself. "I was Rotney."

"So you're saying- you're a player!?" she hops a little as she says it. The slow hiss that you're so familiar with starts escaping from her.

Oh boy, what did she just say about having extreme emotions?

"Oh my god, this is like perfect! You're a player, but a mob, you're exactly what I've been looking for. I love players but I can't get close to them, and now you're here." As she speaks, the hiss grows louder and louder. "Not that I'm saying you like me or anything, that would be crazy, but just you're kind of perfect and I can't believe you're here!"

This is not going to end well.

If you want to run, *turn to page 40!*

If you want to stay close and calm her down, *turn to page 45.*

Man, this isn't worth it. Fibula's the only guy you've got out here anyways.

You "jog" down the hill and catch up with Fibula.

"Sorry," you say, "don't know what I was thinking. I'll come back with you."

"Come back with me?" he stops, "I don't want to hang around with you anymore Rotney. You have a habit of blowing people up."

"But Fibula-"

"No, bye! Find yourself a new home to live in!"

And with that, he wanders off across the hill and away. You're left alone in the valley without a home to go back to for safety during the day.

If you want to continue on the mission and head down the passageway, *turn to page 57.*

If you want to abandon the mission and continue on scaring, *turn to page 54.*

You nod. "I guess you're right," you say. "You won't tell anyone else, right?"

"No, don't worry."

You say goodbye and climb down the ladder of the tree house. You get to the bottom and look up. What a weird, terrible day.

You head off into the dark. It's too hard to go back to the clearing to meet up with the others, they are Teagan's friends after all. And you have to stay away. The only good thing to do is to go off alone.

You choose a new direction and head off.

The morning comes soon and you luckily stumble across a cave before the sun comes back up. You hide there for the day with another zombie and a skeleton. The zombie isn't happy that you're there, stealing her brains, she says. The skeleton seems indifferent, much less talkative than Fibula.

You're worried about going out alone though, so you stay there, day after day. Dreaming of what your life used to be, and wondering about a particular creeper.

THE END

Don't worry though, you can always go back to see what would have happened if you'd tried something else. There are so many different endings you can find if you're clever enough. One of them even will take you to the sequel: Minecraft Zombie Adventure 2: Journey to the Ender.

"Yup, I guess you're right, no players here," you say.

You know how much it sucks to have mobs come after you in this game. You wouldn't want a bunch of them to surprise you in your cool tree fort. If you're going to be on the enemy's side, at least you can help your own guys out. No need to help out these dumb mobs.

You decide that that'll be your own little mission as long as you're here. Keep any of these green skinned weirdoes from getting any of the players. You'll be like a cool double agent!

"What do we do now?" asks Teagan. "Is it worth it to cross the river?"

If you want to cross the river, *turn to page 66.*

If you want to convince Teagan to call it a night, *turn to page 86.*

You head off alone without the skeleton. You wander through couple valleys and biomes before running into another player. This one only has iron armor but still, without Fibula having your back you're in trouble. The player overwhelms you and you drop down into a pit to get away from him.

There's no way out of the pit. The morning comes back and you see the sun light start to cut into the pit. It starts at the far side but as you get to midday the sun fills the whole pit. There's no escape.

The sun gives you one NASTY sunburn. You die.

THE END

Don't worry though, you can always go back to see what would have happened if you'd tried something else. There are so many different endings you can find if you're clever enough. One of them even will take you to the sequel: Minecraft Zombie Adventure 2: Journey to the Ender.

As you watch your mob friends charge forward you realize, a little too late, that this is wrong. You're not a zombie at heart! You're a player! You shouldn't be trying to get this guy eaten, you should be on his side. He's just a noob and needs to be given a chance to learn the game. Minecraft is awesome and you wouldn't want someone to be scared away from the game just because they got mobbed on their first night.

You run towards Fibula. His shot flies through the air and hit the player in the head. Fibula stops shooting and starts rattling forward.

"No! Stop guys! Let's leave this guy alone!" you shout.

"Why?" T-Bone turns around to face you.

"Uuuhhh, you know he's scared already!" you say, unconvincingly.

"Let's finish the job!" shouts Fibula running forward.

You race in front of Fibula and try to stand in front of him. He stops for the moment, he can't get around you.

"What- gah. What are you doing, Rotney? Move!" Fibula is frustrated, trying to clatter around you.

"No Fibula! This player, I think I saw him pull out a diamond sword for a second. He's tricking us! Seriously." Those football practices are coming in handy right now.

"Players don't do that, zombie brains! And we don't care!"

You turn around for a second in the kerfuffle and notice the creepers are rounding the other side of the pillar now. That noob is in trouble! Never mind the skeleton, you set off running. Well, "running", zombie legs, you know. Luckily you still manage to catch up with Teagan and get in front of her. It's not easy to over power her with her tiny legs and no arms.

"Stop! Get out of the way, you bully!" she screams, there's a bit of the terrifying creeper hiss woven into her words.

Fibula shouts from further back, "Rotney, I don't know what's gotten into you, but you better stop getting in our way of eating this guy right now! Mob-code says that if you keep doing that we have to attack you!"

You aren't really listening to Fibula because you can see T-Bone getting awfully close to the player who is trying to punch T-Bone with a flower but keeps punching into the sky instead.

"PLKGUHYFYYHY," the player says.

"Hey, T-Bone! There's like thirty players behind that tree over there!" It's all you can think of to do.

"What?!" says T-Bone. He turns around and tries to find them. Thank goodness that T-Bone is so dumb.

"Alright Rotney! That's it!" shouts Fibula. And you feel something pointy embed itself in your forehead. He's shooting at you!

You turn to the player and yell, "RUUUUNNN!" but it comes out "BLugrRAAAARRRHHH."

"AHHHHH! SCARY ZOMBIE!" the player shouts. He turns to you, and charges.

"No, run away!" you scream.

Another arrow hits you in the back. The player is right in front of you, holding that stupid flower. And somehow he manages to punch you correctly and not mess it up. You're proud for a second and then the pain registers. He punches you again. The world flashes white. You turn into a floating pile of rotting flesh. You're dead.

THE END

Don't worry though, you can always go back to see what would have happened if you'd tried something else. There are so many different endings you can find if you're clever enough. One of them even will take you to the sequel: Minecraft Zombie Adventure 2: Journey to the Ender.

You have a mission and you're determined enough to follow it, you leave Fibula and everyone else behind and dive into the passageway on the hillside. You start down the passageway and its not long before the darkness gives way to a torch. Ten blocks or so farther along there's another one. You can tell that you're closing in on the player. You can smell it.

Before long you enter a room that's about five blocks by five blocks. You see in one corner a chest, a crafting table and in the opposite corner a familiar red bed. On the walls there are many torches. This has to be the player's base. But the player's not here.

You take a look in the chest, piles of iron ore. May iron bars. Some gold- and then you hear a noise behind you. You spin around. The player is standing staring at you from their helmet.

"WHAT THE-"

You are frozen for a second, what were you going to do when you got in here?

"HOW DID YOU GET IN HERE? I BLOCKED IT WITH DIRT, NOT A DOOR, YOU SHOULDN'T BE ABLE TO GET THROUGH. THAT REQUIRES SOME SERIOUS DUMB LUCK. OR SOME SERIOUS INGENUITY..."

You finally overcome your fear and can move again.

If you want to try to bite the player, *turn to page 58*.

If you want to try to communicate to him, *turn to page 98*.

You go in for some of that tasty pizza-flesh.

"OH, I THOUGHT YOU WERE GOING TO BE SOME SORT OF INTERESTING, SMART ZOMBIE, BUT YOU'RE JUST THE SAME AS THE OTHERS."

You miss with your first bite, you go in for another.

"UNLUCKILY FOR YOU, I HAD A COUPLE ROAST CHICKEN HIDDEN IN HERE. AND I'M FEELING MUCH BETTER AFTER A SNACK."

That is not good news. You connect with your second bite. But the delicious taste is only soothing for a second.

With two quick smacks of his diamond sword, you feel the world flash, and go black. You die.

THE END

You don't trust this player enough. Who knows where he could be taking you. And the risk of him punching you out when you least expect it is too high. As far as you know, if you die in here, you don't come back to the real world. You have to play it safe.

You slowly back out of the clearing.

"WHERE ARE YOU GOING?"

You start weaving through the trees.

"ZOMBIE FRIEND?!"

You make your way back to where you started scaring with the others. Before long the creepers and Fibula find their way back to the clearing as well. Fibula asks if any of you had any success. You have to admit: no. He seems pretty disappointed.

"Fine, let's go home," he says.

You walk back but Fibula doesn't talk, he is angry.

You get back to the house you and Fibula share. You try to say goodnight but he just ignores you. You get into your zombie bed. You roll over to sleep, closing your eyes and praying that when you open them again you will be back in your normal skin.

When you do open them again, you aren't. Fibula knocks on your door. "It's scaring time, you pile of rotten flesh."

THE END

"Hey Fibula," you shot down at him, "are there any Endermen around?"

"Endermen?!" Fibula seems shocked. "What do you want with those tall big headed weirdos?!"

"They'd be able to move these blocks," you explain.

"You want to get an Enderman to-" and that's as far as Fibula gets before he breaks down laughing. Skeleton laughter sounds super weird. How to even describe it? It's like if a really old vacuum cleaner was running while surrounded by a bunch of laughing hyenas accompanied by an orchestra of five year olds on drum sets. Yeah, unpleasant.

When Fibula finally gets his breath back he says, "There's no convincing an Enderman to do anything. They are very weird, aloof creatures Rotney. They'll hardly talk to anyone else."

"Well can you at least show me to them! I want to give it a try!" you say.

"You're a lunatic Rotney. And this is crazy anyways. The player is gone. We got him back into hiding, which was our goal! We're going to have bragging rights for a while with the rest of the mobs! Let's go."

"Come on Fibula. You owe me one."

He stops and looks back.

"I saved your life," you say.

He pauses.

"My death," he says.

"What?" you ask.

"You saved my death. I'm a skeleton. Undead, remember?"

You smile. Or at least you try to smile. Can zombies smile?

"But you're right, I do owe you. Let's go find you an Enderman!" he says as he takes you further down the valley.

"Endermen are tricky," he explains as you go, "they don't really ever stay in the same place for very long, what with the teleportation and all."

You nod, that makes sense.

"But, they do have a special interest in anything that's pretty, so you can often find them congregating in particular places. Like up here." He takes you up to the top of a plateau. "There's a waterfall across from here and I think they just like watching it. Weirdos."

As you get to the top of the plateau, you have a question. "So what, should we not look at them, if we do find an Enderman?"

"No," Fibula answers, "That's just a player thing mostly. We all hate players. Well, most of us. So any little provocation can really set an Enderman off and they'll go all crazy weird teleporty attack on a player. But they don't like being looked at too much anyways. Even by one of us. So just keep your eyes down and don't try to maintain too much eye contact. And don't even ASK me how to get them to move some blocks for you. But I said I'd take you to them."

He did, and he is successful. In the center of the plateau sounds a tall, gangly, Enderman, it's looking around, pivoting, holding a block of dirt like it's the Enderman's baby. Okay, here we go.

You walk up to it, keeping your gaze low, and as you get close the Enderman pivots around and seems to notice you. You glance up for a split second and see it staring inquisitively.

"Um hello, Mr. Enderman sir. How- are you?"

"Portia." The Enderman's voice sounds ancient and otherworldly. Like it were singing up to you from inside a crypt.

"What?" you look up at it and then remember and revert your gaze back down again.

"My name's Portia."

"Oh, hi, I'm Rotney." You keep looking down.

"Why don't you look at me?"

"Um, I didn't want to offend you or anything." You look back at Fibula but he just shrugs his shoulder bones and hops back a block.

"You can look at me."

You look up at her, her purple eyes are boring into your pixelated, undead soul.

"Don't stare," she says, less sing-songy now.

You drop your gaze back down. There's silence. She teleports right behind you. It's very shocking.

"Well, what did you think?" she asks from behind you. You can still feel her watching you.

"Um, very… black. Tall. Long arms." You mentally smack yourself in the forehead, what stupid things to say!

She seems sulky and wanders away a little, going back to staring at the waterfall.

What are you going to do? You need to figure out how to get Portia to come back with you down the valley to the blocks so that she can remove them. These Endermen do seem like weird creatures and you only know a couple things about them. They don't like staring. You could get her down the valley by staring at her and provoking her to follow you in a rage. It might work?

If you want to compliment Portia's appearance, *turn to page 64.*

If you want to lure her down the valley by staring, *turn to page 44.*

"Falling's not the only thing that hurts," you growl and go in for the bite. SCRUNCH. You bite into him and your mouth fills with the succulent tastes of... bacon pizza! Wow, eating people is kind of awesome. When you're a zombie. Please don't go eating people in your real life.

"AHHHHHH" the player says. "A GREEN VERSION OF ME IS HURTING ME! I HATE THIS GAME!"

You go in for another bite; this time it tastes like ice cream sundaes. Hot fudge, particularly.

"HOW DO I PUNCH STUFF?!"

The player flashes and then disappears. Those were great last words.

Driven by the hunger for player flesh you wander around the rest of the night looking for people to eat. The noob respawns nearby and you eat him again. And then again.

And once more.

And then you guess he finally stopped playing the game. Which is a shame. But it was so fun while it lasted!

You meet back up with the others and tell them how you had such a good time scaring. That's good, none of them had a lot of success. You embrace your zombie-ness. Night after night you go out and eat people. The hunger for flesh is just so addictive! You've become a true zombie.

THE END

Don't worry though, you can always go back to see what would have happened if you'd tried something else. There are so many different endings you can find if you're clever enough. One of them even will take you to the sequel: Minecraft Zombie Adventure 2: Journey to the Ender.

You've got a crazy idea. You start putting some of the things that Fibula said together. You know that they don't like being looked at, but why is that? Are they just shy? Fibula would say it's just because they're weirdos, but there's got to be something else.

What if they don't like being looked at because they're self conscious? You think back to that one day in grade one after your mom gave you a haircut. She literally just put a bowl on your head and cut around it in a circle, no wonder all the kids called you 'bowl-head' all day. That day you didn't want anyone to speak to you or even look at you all day. You wish you had had an invisibility cloak or could just shrink down to the size of a penny or something. Maybe it was the same with the Endermen!

Fibula said that they really appreciated beauty! Like that waterfall! If they're so interested in beauty maybe it's because they don't feel like they're beautiful themselves. That must be hard. It's worth a try.

You wander over to Portia who is staring off the side of the plateau. You stand beside her for a second and watch the waterfall as well. It truly is gorgeous, huge, as tall as a mountain and wide too. You watch a couple blocks floating in the stream pour over the edge and land in the sea below. You wonder what could have put them there.

"The waterfall is quite pretty," you say. You can see just enough of Portia out of the side of your eyes to watch her nod. "The second most beautiful thing in this mountain range," you continue.

Portia looks around madly, swivelling on the spot at an incredible pace. "I don't think so," she says finally.

"Oh, I do," you say, trying to control your smile.

Portia looks right at you. "What's more beautiful? I don't see anything."

"Right, sorry," you say, "I guess you wouldn't. You can't see it."

"Invisible waterfall?" she asks, excited.

"No, its you! You're the first most beautiful thing, and then the waterfall."

She teleports three times, around you. Out of excitement, you guess. "You are very kind. And you turn my cheeks red."

You look up at her, you don't think that Mojang's programming actually lets Endermen blush. "Nobody would notice," you say.

She puts down her block and doesn't seem to mind you looking now. "Thank you, Rotney."

"Oh, I had a favor to ask you, if you have a second. I need a couple blocks moved down in the valley," you say.

"Of course," she says, "show me where!" She teleports to the other edge of the plateau, near Fibula and strides down into the valley. You hurry after. As you pass Fibula, he gives you a high five. It's a bit awkward with your hands stuck out in front of your face.

You all go to the place of the player's escape and Portia happily removes the blocks and makes a little stack in the middle of the valley. She also tells you that all of life takes place in the center of a daffodil and that she lived another life as a pig, none of it makes any sense.

"Are you really going to go?" Fibula asks. "It's getting early and I think I'm going to head back home."

"Does the nice zombie have to go?" Portia sings.

If you want to stay here with Fibula and Portia, *turn to page 69.*

If you want to enter the passageway, *turn to page 57.*

You guys approach the river, its flowing strongly from right to left.

"You sure this is a good idea?" Teagan asks.

"Yeah, sure," you say, "we'll just swim to the other side if it's too deep."

You guys stride into the river. Well Teagan doesn't so much stride as waddle and you don't so much stride as stumble. You take a couple steps in and watch a couple floating blocks caught up in the current flow past. A couple more steps and it's get too deep, you'll have to swim it. Before you can decide if that's a good idea or not, the current makes the decision for you. You're floating down the river, and Teagan's bobbing behind you.

You try to swim forward and then realize that you're a mob. And mobs are really bad at swimming. It's still possible though, just going to be slow going.

"Come on," you shout to Teagan, "to the other side!"

You keep paddling and bobbing forward, but it's not quick and soon you notice a cave coming up on your left. The river's flowing into it! The current sweeps you inside and then mysteriously the river stops. Well, it doesn't stop, the current keeps going strong, but the water must go underground or something at this point, because there's no way out of the cave besides the way you came in and the current keeps pulling you against the back wall of the cave. There's not even any land to get out on the side of the river. The river goes right up to the edge of the cave. You guys are in trouble. If only mobs could dive down like players!

It's then that you notice the crowd of other mobs, skeletons, zombies, creepers, spiders, even a zombie pig man bobbing against the back wall of the cave. As you and Teagan get sucked into the back of the cave, the other's greet you.

"Howdy."

"Hi."

"Come on in."

"Welcome to the eternity cave," says the zombie pig man. "You've come to a good place, we are friendly here. Tell us your story."

"Tell us your story!" the others chant back.

You sit there bobbing against two skeletons. "Ummm, we tried to cross the river and then we got sucked by the current into this cave and can't get out," you say.

"Hey, that's just like my story!" shouts a nearby skeleton.

"Me too!"

"Me three!"

"This guy stole my story!"

"Well my story is different," says a zombie at the back. Everyone turns in attention. "I got PUSHED into the river and then got sucked by the current into this cave and can't get out."

The crowd oooos and ahhhs and claps.

Then everyone bobs in silence for a second.

Oh boy. This is going to be a boring place to spend the rest of eternity.

"This was a terrible idea. We should have never crossed the river, genius," Teagan whispers to you. "I hate you, zombie brains."

"Hey, new zombie, tell us your story again, it was a good one," says the pig man.

"We tried to cross the river and then we got sucked by the current into this cave and can't get out," you say.

"Hey, that's just like my story!" shouts the same skeleton.

You sigh.

THE END

Don't worry though, you can always go back to see what would have happened if you'd tried something else. There are so many different endings you can find if you're clever enough. One of them even will take you to the sequel: Minecraft Zombie Adventure 2: Journey to the Ender.

You look at the passageway and then walk back down the hill to the skeleton and Enderman. That player can just be left alone. Suddenly the urge to go after the player doesn't feel as strong. You're kind of happy being here with Fibula and Portia.

Fibula speaks up "Hey guys, I think we did a good job for tonight. Let's just head home."

You head back over the hill to the clearing where you meet up with T-Dawg, Portia trails along. You don't mind. She's entertaining if nothing else.

All of you head back to the home where you and Fibula started. Fibula starts telling the others about your daring moves against the player earlier! You were a hero and saved him. The others ooo and aww as they hear about your vicious bites and quick thinking. Portia looks at you admiringly.

You get back to the cave that you and Fibula seem to call home and you snuggle into bed for the day. Fibula appears at the door of you room. "Good work out there."

"Thanks," you say.

You fall asleep and the next night you get up and go scaring again.

And you fall asleep and do the same thing the next night.

And the night after.

You're a Minecraft zombie now and it's not so bad after all.

THE END

Don't worry though, you can always go back to see what would have happened if you'd tried something else. There are so many different endings you can find if you make the right choices. One of them even will take you to the sequel: Minecraft Zombie Adventure 2: Journey to the Ender.

There's just something about those woods that you can't ignore. Have you ever gotten one of those urges to do something that you totally can't explain? Because it's like that.

You head off alone to the woods. Nobody follows you and nobody's with you.

It really is a strange feeling. It's like having a hunch, but with a direction. Maybe, you think, it's the zombie part of you speaking. That would explain why its so alien and strange. Maybe a part of this zombie brain you have found yourself inside of has a feeling about going in this direction. But why?

The trees are dense here. Sometimes you have to double back and go around some trees to make your way forward. In the distance you hear something peculiar, there's some sort of crunch-crunch noise that you can almost make out.

You think again about why there is this strange tug, pulling you forward. And then you realize, maybe this is what zombie hunger feels like! Now that you're a zombie do you have the ability to detect players and their tasty, tasty flesh! At first you think this is pretty cool, I mean imagine having this extra ability to sense people. Then you realize that you only have that sense because you want to eat their brains. That's a little less cool. Your zombie stomach grumbles.

Your zombie sense is urging you to find something in this next clearing. There's a large tree in your way and you just wish that you could punch the thing down. You try for a second but your zombie hands hit the hard wood of the tree like floppy fish. *Sploop Shquish.* Fine. You guess you'll just have to walk around.

As you round the corner, your hunger grows, this is where it's been dragging you! And there it is. You see it in the clearing. It's a weird tower. One block wide, sticking straight out of the ground. Wait, do you have the ability to sense stupid dirt towers? That's the worst ability of all time, no offence.

And then you look up and realize what's standing on top of that tower: a player. He's jumping up and down, stupidly, and looking around. He has a flower in his hand, not even a tool. And the skin of his character you realize is just the default:

brown hair, teal shirt, blue pants. You know what this is, you would know it anywhere. Heck, you were once one yourself, how could you not recognize it? That's a noob. And the thing he's standing on is a noob tower.

'What a dummy," you think to yourself, 'he wasn't even good enough to make a house on the first night, couldn't get a bed, or even spend the night mining like any good player does. Instead, he had to stay outside through the night, and to protect himself he's built a tower that he's stranded on top of, but at least the mobs can't get him. That is, until he meets a skeleton.'

You would put your palm to your forehead if they weren't stuck out in front of you. You realize that his tower is probably not even tall enough to protect him from a creeper. It would just blow up at the the bottom of his tower. This poor sucker is just asking to be eaten!

It would be so satisfying to get the whole team of mobs over here and teach him a lesson, you'd just have to call them, they'd be so proud of you! But he is just a noob, everyone starts that way, maybe he deserves to be saved…

If you want to call the rest of the mobs over, *turn to page 91*.

If you want to keep it a secret and approach by yourself, *turn to page 90*.

This poor noob is going to get what's coming to him! It's just so easy. Huh, maybe being a zombie is kind of fun.

"FIBULA! TEAGAN! T-BONE! There's a noob over here to be scared!" you shout! It's sounds just ghastly coming out of your mouth in your normal zombie groans and grunts.

"HEY, WHAT ARE YOU SAYING?" says the noob. "WHAT DO THOSE MOANS MEAN?"

When he speaks the world kind of shakes a little and all his words show up floating in the sky as white letters. Silly player.

"HELLO?" Aw, the poor guy.

It's not long before a green shape shows up beside you suddenly. It's T-Bone.

"Woah! I didn't see you coming!" you jump a little.

"I blend into the forest," he says. Good point.

To highlight the point, you look on your other side to see Teagan standing there. You jump again! Teagan laughs at you.

"So, what's going on?" she asks, once she can control her giggles.

"Oh, there's a noob over there. Look!" You point at the noob who's now just wandering around the base of his tower

"OH MY MOD!" screams T-Bone, "A player!" He tries to run forward but just bumps into the trees.

Just then you hear a familiar clatter and Fibula is there!

"A noob on a noob tower?!" he says. "Best day ever! Let's go!"

You round the trees with the creepers and the skeleton and the creepers charge forward while Fibula starts shooting at the player.

"UH OH. THIS AIN'T GOOD," says the noob. "WHAT ARE THE WEIRD

GREEN PILLARS WITH FEET AGAIN?"

Aw man, this guy knows nothing about the game at all, he's about to be blown out of the water. You do feel a little bad about it, that was you once after all.

If you want to stop the mobs and save the noob, *turn to page 55*.

If you want to join them in the scaring, *turn to page 80*.

You arrive back in the plains where you started the scaring with T and T and Fibula. The moon hangs heavy in the sky, the darkness has settled on the land, but you can see through it as if it were the middle of the day. Zombie legs might be terrible but zombie eyes have their upside.

You see T-Dawg in the corner still bumping into the sides of a cliff, he's really not very smart. A big jelly sits nearby him, plopping along lazily. Those things usually give you the creeps when you're playing, but now, you realize, they can't do anything to you. The night is safe, except for those no-good players.

To your left you see the hills that Fibula went over. In front of you is the way to the river. And on the right is the big forest. Its trees loom over you uneasily. Something calls to you from the forest.

If you want to go to the river, *turn to page 21*.

If you want to go to the woods, *turn to page 70*.

"Let's check out the tree, seems like a place that I would hide out when I-" Oops. You've said too much, you don't want to freak out the creeper.

Teagan is trailing behind you. "When you what?"

Uh oh, think fast. You better figure this one out. Come on!

"When I was playing hide and seek with T-Dawg," you say. That was close.

"You guys play hide and seek?! That seems dangerous, I feel like if he ever found you it could get pretty dangerous. He'd get so excited that, kablooey, you know?"

'Creepers explode when they get excited?' you think. But you say, "Find me? T-Dawg never found me, come on."

Teagan laughs her hissy, scary laugh. She's going to kill you with that thing. You promise yourself that you'll never make her laugh again.

"Yeah, my brother might not be the sharpest axe in the chest." Apparently that's a saying here.

"I think it's worse than that: he's a shovel in a chest of axes," you say.

She laughs. You broke your promise right away!

You guys have gotten to the tree now and you look up, there is a faint light, you think, coming from the top of this massive weird tree. Its trunk is three blocks wide and it extends maybe ten or twenty blocks into the air with lots of foliage. It's really quite a marvellous tree.

Teagan does a little tour of the outside of the tree. "No players, I guess," she says, but doesn't seem too upset. You think about the light at the top of the tree, she's probably wrong.

If you want to tell her about the light, *turn to page 78.*

If you want to let her think there's no one around, *turn to page 53.*

You run forward with the creepers. That hunger that was pulling you this direction from the beginning is throbbing in your stomach now.

Fibula's first shot lands. It hits the player, but he isn't dead yet. He's still ripe for the eating, you just have to get there before these creepers. You shoulder-check Teagan.

"Hey!" she shouts, falling over.

"T-Bone, that tree over there wants to give you a leg bump!" you say.

"What really?" He spins around looking for the tree. If he was a player he'd probably try to dig through bedrock.

You get around the pillar first and see the player staring up into the air. You dive in! CHOMP! You take a big bite out of the player. It's delicious. You try to place the flavor: bacon pizza. With added sausage. The player flashes but doesn't blow up into his inventory.

Time for another bite! The second bite tastes a little more like ice cream sundaes covered in Nutella. Amazing! This bite gets him. Blocks of dirt, saplings and raw pork chops explode everywhere.

Fibula let's out a little woop behind you! He rushes up and gives you a bony hug. Even the creepers seem pleased and congratulate you.

"Sorry about the tricks guys," you say, "I just didn't want to get blown up."

Teagan smiles at you. "Yeah, don't worry I get it. Nice going!"

T-Bone says, "Yeah good work Rotney. But where was that tree that wanted a leg bump?"

The others laugh. You do too.

"Okay, I think that's pretty good for the night," says Fibula, "We can brag about that to the mobs in the next chunk over for a while. Let's head home."

The four of you start walking back. You pass a jelly along the way and Fibula tells him about how awesome you were back there. You can't help but blush a little. You wonder what a zombie blush looks like.

It's not so bad, really, being a zombie. You've got good friends. Players are delicious, who knew? You might be happy here for a while until you can figure out how to get back home.

You get back to the house you and Fibula share. You say good bye to T and T. You crawl into bed and Fibula peeks into your room.

"Goodnight," he says, "see you tomorrow night."

"Tomorrow night," you say. And roll over for a blink of zombie sleep.

THE END

Don't worry though, you can always go back to see what would have happened if you'd tried something else. There are so many different endings you can find if you're clever enough. One of them even will take you to the sequel: Minecraft Zombie Adventure 2: Journey to the Ender.

"Actually," you say, "there's a light at the top of the tree. You see? Probably a torch. A player would have had to put it up there."

"Oh my Mod, Rotney, you are SO smart. Zombies are not supposed to be smart, man. Where did you learn stuff like that?"

"Oh," you say, "well, let's just say that I'm good at thinking as if I were a player."

She gives you this really weird luck. It's admiration, you think. Or maybe she's on to you?

"Check out these weird mini-trees," she says from the other side of the tree.

You wander around the other side to see what she's talking about. She's standing there staring at something brown running up the side of the trunk.

"And they've got branches going from one to the other. I see these things all over the place. Trees are weird," she continues.

You laugh a little. "That's a ladder."

"A ladder?" She seems confused.

"Yeah, a ladder." She doesn't seem to know what you're talking about. I guess creepers don't know about ladders. They never use them in the game! You guess it makes sense. "It's like a sideways fence? You use it to go up."

"Like jumping?"

"Um, no," you say. "Let me show you."

Your zombie arms are a little useless at climbing but as long as you keep walking forward in the direction of the ladder, you slowly climb up it. Once you're up a couple blocks you hop back down. Teagan looks like you've just done a magic trick. Her big, open, creeper mouth is even bigger and more open.

"Rotney B. Zombie," she say, "you are full of surprises!" She seems so genuinely excited, it makes you excited too. "I wish creepers could do that," she continues.

"Oh, oh, they can, you can!" you say. She comes over to try it and is delighted when she rises a couple blocks up into the air.

"Oh my Mod, Rotney, this is amazing!" Teagan exclaims. "Well, I guess with this we can go up there to get the player, can't we?"

You guess so. What else can you say?

You lead the way up the ladder and Teagan follows you up the ladder. The ladder goes straight up the side of the tree and as you get further up you can see a platform built of wooden planks is perched above the leaves. You've made a treehouse like this plenty of time while you were playing the game.

Then a sound of a furnace burning away, a sound you wouldn't miss anywhere, carries down from overhead. There really is a player up there. A player who is about to get his avatar's pants scared off when a zombie and a creeper climb up his ladder and surprise him. Either you or him is not going to make it out of this meeting. Is this worth it?

If you'd like to stop climbing up the ladder, *turn to page 34.*

If you want to keep going, *turn to page 41.*

You run forward with the creepers. That hunger that was pulling you this direction from the beginning is throbbing in your stomach now.

Fibula's first shot lands. It hits the player, but he isn't dead yet. He's still ripe for the eating, you just have to get there before these creepers. You shoulder-check Teagan.

"Hey!" she shouts, falling over.

"T-Bone, that tree over there wants to give you a leg bump!" you say.

"What really?" He spins around looking for the tree. If he was a player he'd probably try to dig through bedrock.

You get around the pillar first and see the player staring up into the air. You dive in! CHOMP! You take a big bite out of the player. It's delicious. You try to place the flavor: bacon pizza. With added sausage. The player flashes but doesn't blow up into his inventory.

Time for another bite! The second bite tastes a little more like ice cream sundaes covered in Nutella. Amazing! This bite gets him. Blocks of dirt, saplings and raw pork chops explode everywhere.

Fibula let's out a little woop behind you! He rushes up and gives you a bony hug. Even the creepers seem pleased and congratulate you.

"Sorry about the tricks guys," you say, "I just didn't want to get blown up."

Teagan smiles at you. "Yeah, don't worry I get it. Nice going!"

T-Bone says, "Yeah good work Rotney. But where was that tree that wanted a leg bump?"

The others laugh. You do too.

"Okay, I think that's pretty good for the night," says Fibula, "We can brag about that to the mobs in the next chunk over for a while. Let's head home."

The four of you start walking back. You pass a jelly along the way and Fibula tells him about how awesome you were back there. You can't help but blush a little. You wonder what a zombie blush looks like.

It's not so bad, really, being a zombie. You've got good friends. Players are delicious, who knew? You might be happy here for awhile until you can figure out how to get back home.

You get back to the house you and Fibula share. You say good bye to T and T. You crawl into bed and Fibula peeks into your room.

"Goodnight," he says, "see you tomorrow night."

"Tomorrow night," you say. And roll over for a blink of zombie sleep.

THE END

Don't worry though, you can always go back to see what would have happened if you'd tried something else. There are so many different endings you can find if you're clever enough. One of them even will take you to the sequel: Minecraft Zombie Adventure 2: Journey to the Ender.

"Pardon me, but it just doesn't sound great," you say. "I'm not an expert on reading creeper emotions, but that's not the sort of way people- mobs, normally say 'great'."

She kind of looks away, but is silent.

"I mean maybe its just that 'great' means something different in creeper, I'm no expert," you say. "Maybe 'great' means like: super terrible and sad. Maybe you all go to funerals and go over to each other and say 'this is great, it's great this guy is dead.' Getting the flu is great! It's great when a truck drives by and splashes you with dirty puddle water!"

You hear a little hissy laugh which she's trying to muffle.

"Okay, you're right, I don't feel great about it," she says.

"Why not? Isn't this what you guys, I mean, we, us mobs, are all about?" Way to go there, you almost let it slip, dumby. "We chase players, we want them to run away and blow up or stupidly jump a hundred blocks out of a treehouse and hit the ground and have their items splatter everywhere!"

"Well, I know, that's what we're supposed to be into. That's what Fibula is into for sure. And you too. All skeletons and zombies love that stuff." Teagan looks embarrassed. "We try not to talk about it too much, but us creepers just aren't so interested in any of that. We don't mention it because we don't want you guys to think that we're weird."

This is news. You wonder if Fibula knows about this. "But I don't understand," you say, "you guys seem into the scaring going out and finding players. Why do you do it if you don't even like it?"

"Well, I never said that we don't like going out to find the players," she says. "We just don't like the whole blowing up, eating or shooting thing. We still like the hunt. That's why I'm out here."

"I don't get it… If you're not trying to scare the players, what do you want to do to them when you find them?"

Teagan looks up at you with a silly look on her green face. "Get a hug? I know it sounds dumb, and I'm kidding. Kinda."

You just stare at her in disbelief.

"Have you ever seen a player?" she asks.

"Yeah, sure." If only she knew how silly of a question that is!

"Seriously, I've never talked with a non-creeper about this, but there's something special about you today Rotney. If you've seen one then maybe you know, they're… they're just so great. Right?"

What now?

She continues. "Players are so smart. When they talk, the world rumbles with their words. They can create things and destroy them. They can build beautiful structures. They don't just wander around the world bumping into things like us. They're so powerful! They're like wizards! They're almost- gods… And when you see one, it's so hard to stop yourself from just walking over and trying to get as close as possible to those wonderful creatures. And when we get close we creepers just get so excited, to be near a real-life player!"

"Why are you guys always blowing us- them up, then?" Luckily you don't think she notices your mess up in her excitement.

"Well, creepers aren't very good at dealing with their emotions. Sadness, fear, anger, excitement, if any of them get too strong- well. You know."

You look at her. She makes a very convincing explosion sound with her mouth. You jump. She smiles a weird creeper smile, you didn't know the devs had even programmed that into the game. There's something about this creeper you really, really like.

"Do you hate me?" she asks.

"Hate you? Why would I hate you?"

"I feel like a normal zombie wouldn't be so cool that creepers are in love with their sworn enemy."

"Normal zombie! What are you saying about me?" you say, trying to keep up the act.

"Well, I don't think it's a surprise that you're a bit weird as zombies go. At least today."

"I don't know what you're talking about." You don't know if you were quite convincing on that one.

"Oh come on. You've been all... smart today. You noticed light up here so you knew there were people around, that's not like a zombie, not like any mob. You knew how to climb ladders! Heck, you know what ladders are! That's weird. For any mob. But especially for a zombie. No offence."

"A little offence taken," you say.

"You know what it's like actually?" she asks, but she doesn't wait for an answer, "It's kinda like a player. You've been kind of player-y today actually."

You shift around a bit uncomfortably. You let out a zombie moan to make a point.

"That's why I like you so much today!" she looks at you. But you look away. You like the attention, but you don't know what to say, should you tell her? Will she think you're crazy? Are you crazy? You think you're a Minecraft zombie! She seems to be waiting for you to say something.

"How'd you get so smart?" she says, breaking the awkward silence.

"Well, I do eat a LOT of brains," you say.

She laughs her scary, yet cute, laugh.

"Okay," she says, "I've told you my weird embarrassing secret, your turn! What haven't you told anybody?"

Uh oh.

"Come on, it's only fair," she says, expectantly.

John Diary

If you want to tell her that you're a player stuck in a zombie's body, *turn to page 49.*

If you want to tell her that you like her too, *turn to page 35.*

"Eh, I don't know," you say. "The water seems to be flowing kind of quick. Maybe we just call it a night. There doesn't seem to be any players around. And you know what? I'm not really feeling into it." You cross your fingers. Wait, you don't have fingers. You pretend to cross your imaginary fingers.

"Hmmm," she says, "really? You love scaring people."

"Just not feeling it tonight. If you really want to, we can keep going though. I mean, if that's what you want." You have a hunch here, and want to follow it.

"No, I don't really want to…" she says. "Just tonight, not like in general or anything."

"Sure," you say. "Let's go back to the clearing and see if we can find the others."

"Sounds good," she says, following you back.

You guys get back to where you started scaring. T-Dawg is there, a jelly plops along beside him. You guys can't find Fibula, but together you walk back to the home where you and Fibula started.

Night after night, you go out with the other mobs. You distract them. You warn away players. You throw the other mobs off the scent. You lead everyone on wild goose chases after imaginary players. You're a silent, unknown hero. But as the nights pass you save more heroes than you can count.

It's a strange existence, but at least you're doing the right thing.

One time, months after that first, strange night, you overhear two players speaking in a cave that you're guarding from other mobs.

"I THINK THAT'S THE HERO ZOMBIE," one of them says to the other.

"WHO?"

"YOU HAVEN'T HEARD ABOUT THE HERO ZOMBIE? IT MIGHT JUST BE A RUMOUR, BUT THEY SAY THERE'S A ZOMBIE ON THIS SERVER WHO'S PROGRAMMED TO PROTECT YOU DURING THE NIGHT. NOT

EAT YOU."

"THAT'S STUPID. NOTCH WOULD NEVER PROGRAM THAT. JUST NOOB TALK."

"YEAH, SURE. PROBABLY. BUT THERE'S ALWAYS BEEN SOMETHING UP WITH THIS SERVER. IT'S BECAUSE IT'S SO OLD. IT'S GOT QUIRKS."

The sun comes up and you scamper away. But you can't stop smiling. They know you! You have a name! A legend!

You miss your family, and your old life, but somehow that makes it a little bit worth it.

THE END

Congratulations! You made it to the end. But, you can always go back to see what would have happened if you'd tried something else. There are so many different endings you can find if you're clever enough. One of them even will take you to the sequel: Minecraft Zombie Adventure 2: Journey to the Ender.

"Hello? Rotney?!" he keeps calling out to you. But his voice is fading now. He must be walking away. Phew!

The player starts moving again.

"OKAY, I HAVE A MORSE CODE CHART. WHY ARE YOU A ZOMBIE THAT CAN SPEAK MORSE CODE?"

"Finally!" you hop out in Morse code, "I am a player like you, but I'm stuck in the body of this zombie. I need your help."

It takes a while but the player decodes it.

"OKAY. YEAH, BUT THAT SOUNDS TOTALLY CRAZY."

"Well, you are talking in Morse code to a Minecraft zombie. Things are already pretty crazy," you hop out.

He checks his chart. Then, finally:

"GOOD POINT. OKAY WHAT CAN I DO?"

You tell him that you need him to look up if there is anything on the internet about someone getting stuck like this. He says he'll go look. Again, you wait, holding your breath until he comes back.

"BAD NEWS, NO HELPFUL WIKI PAGE ABOUT GETTING STUCK IN MINECRAFT."

You don't have any time for jokes, this is your life!

"BUT, I DID FIND A STORY SOMEONE PUBLISHED ABOUT THIS PARTICULAR SERVER, DID YOU KNOW THAT IT'S THE OLDEST SERVER EVER? ANYWAYS SOMEONE WROTE A STORY ABOUT SOMEONE GETTING STUCK IN THIS SERVER IN THE BODY OF A MOB. AND THEY MANAGED TO GET BACK OUT."

"That's great," you hop excitedly!

"BUT IT'S JUST A STORY."

"Maybe, but it's all that we have. How did they get out, we have to do the same thing."

"LET ME CHECK."

And then after a second.

"THEY STARTED BY TALKING TO A MOB NEARBY TO HERE. FOLLOW ME."

If you want to follow him, *turn to page 106*.

If you want to go back to the others, *turn to page 59*.

This player isn't going to be a threat. And he might need to be let off easy anyways.

You come out of the trees. But the player is facing the other direction. You watch him squat on the tower and then stand. Squat. Stand. Squat, stand.

Maybe you made a mistake. Maybe it's not a noob. Maybe there's a chimpanzee at a computer.

"HOW DO YOU BUILD SIDEWAYS WHILE YOU'RE STANDING ON SOMETHING?" he says to the world at large.

Well, the chimpanzee speaks English, it seems. The player scoots to the edge of the block with a cube of dirt in his hand. And then he just falls off the side.

"DAMN. DOES FALLING HURT YOU?" the noob says.

This guy is kind of getting on your nerves, maybe it is best to eat him? I mean, once he sees you isn't he just going to start punching you?

If you want to eat the player, *turn to page 63*.

If you want to befriend him, *turn to page 95*.

This poor noob is going to get what's coming to him! It's just so easy. Huh, maybe being a zombie is kind of fun.

"FIBULA! TEAGAN! T-BONE! There's a noob over here to be scared!" you shout! It's sounds just ghastly coming out of your mouth in your normal zombie groans and grunts.

"HEY, WHO'S THERE?" says the noob. "WHAT'S THAT? THERE'S WEIRD MONSTER NOISES COMING FROM THE FOREST! SOMEONE HELP!"

When he speaks the world kind of shakes a little and all his words show up floating in the sky as white letters.

"SOMEBODY?" Aw, the poor guy.

It's not long before a green shape shows up beside you suddenly. It's T-Bone.

"Woah! I didn't see you coming!" you jump a little.

"I blend into the forest," he says. Good point.

To highlight the point, you look on your other side to see Teagan standing there. You jump again! Teagan laughs at you.

"So, what's going on?" she asks, once she can control her giggles.

"Oh, there's a noob over there. He built a noob tower and is just standing on top of it. Look!" You point through the woods.

"OH MY MOD!" screams T-Bone, "A player!" He tries to run forward but just bumps into the trees.

Just then you hear a familiar clatter and Fibula is there!

"A noob on a noob tower?!" he says. "Best day ever! Let's go!"

You round the trees with the creepers and the skeleton and the creepers charge forward while Fibula starts shooting at the player. His first shot lands and the player gets pushed back and falls off the tower.

"UH OH. THIS AIN'T GOOD," says the noob. "WHAT ARE THE WEIRD GREEN PILLARS WITH FEET AGAIN?"

Aw man, this guy knows nothing about the game at all, he's about to be blown out of the water. You do feel a little bad about it, that was you once after all.

If you want to stop the mobs and save the noob, *turn to page 55*.

If you want to join them in the scaring, *turn to page 80*.

"Oh hey T-Bone! I'm over here! But haven't found anything," you shout, "Let's meet back at the clearing. Whoever gets there first gets a leg bump!"

"Oh hey buddy!" T-Bone calls through the trees. "No worries, I'll walk you back, I'd love to chat."

Oh no, not good.

"And you know you can get a leg bump for free from me anytime!" he continues.

You hear him coming closer.

"There you are!" He pokes out of the trees. And then he sees the player standing still. "And there you aaarrreee…"

He trails off as he starts walking in a trance towards the player.

"OKAY, I HAVE A MORSE CODE CHART. WHY ARE YOU A ZOMBIE THAT CAN SPEAK- OH BOY YOU'VE GOT A FRIEND!"

You try to step between T-Bone and the player.

"HI GREEN PILLAR WITH LEGS! DO YOU SPEAK MORSE CODE TOO?"

T-Bone is an unstoppable force, he keeps moving as much as you try to slow him down.

"WHAT'S HAPPENING?" the player asks.

You don't have time to hop anything out for this guy, why won't he just run! As much as you walk against T-Bone, his attraction to the player is too strong and he keeps pushing you further and further back. Far enough back that he starts making that familiar hiss.

Uh oh.

"WHAT'S THAT?"

"Plaayyyyeerrrrr…" T-Bone drools.

KABOOOOOOM!

You die.

THE END

Don't worry though, you can always go back to see what would have happened if you'd tried something else. There are so many different endings you can find if you're clever enough. One of them even will take you to the sequel: Minecraft Zombie Adventure 2: Journey to the Ender.

The noob turns and sees you.

"OH." He doesn't seem nervous that there's a zombie right beside him.

"ARE YOU A ZOMBIE?"

"Um, yeah," you say, but then realize how stupid that is.

"WHY AM I TALKING TO A ZOMBIE? DO ZOMBIES TALK, GUYS?"

It seems like whatever players he seems to think he's talking to aren't responding. Maybe they're just annoyed. The guy kind of is annoying. Maybe you should eat him after all? It would be easy enough to get all the mobs over here to give him a scare.

If you want to call the other mobs over to eat him, *turn to page 72*.

If you want to try to talk to him, *turn to page 96*.

How are you going to communicate with this guy?

"WELL, I GUESS YOU PROBABLY CAN'T TALK. BUT THANKS FOR NOT EATING ME ZOMBIE. YOU SEEM LIKE A SPECIAL ZOMBIE, BECAUSE YOU'RE NOT ATTACKING ME."

If only you could tell this kid that you needed help. He has access to a phone, he has access to Google! Maybe he could figure out a way to get you out of this mess.

And that's when you have a brain wave: you start hopping. First you hop quickly three times. Then three times slowly. And then another three hops quickly again.

"WOW, YOU'RE A JUMPY ZOMBIE. WHAT DOES THIS MEAN?"

You keep doing it. Hop, hop, hop! Hop. Hop. Hop. Hop, hop, hop!

"UM, IS THIS A GLITCH?" He looks around.

'No, come on,' you think. 'Nooby, it's Morse code!' You don't have hands to do sign language, or fingers to write, but you can still tap out the old code that people used to communicate with each other on early radios, before phones. Who would have thought you would need to use such an old technology to free yourself from being stuck in a brand new one.

He looks at you again, and watches you jump the same pattern.

"OH, WAIT. ISN'T THAT S.O.S. OR SOMETHING?"

You nod your head vigorously, looking up then down. Up then down.

"I DON'T BELIEVE THIS! YOU CAN TALK!" the player is so excited! "CAN YOU UNDERSTAND ME?"

You nod your head again.

You hop out "I need your help," in Morse code. It's a good thing your grandpa made you learn it on those long boring Sunday afternoons.

"WAIT, WHAT? I DON'T KNOW ANYTHING ELSE BESIDE S.O.S."

Look it up dummy.

"I GUESS I COULD LOOK IT UP."

There we go.

"BUT WHAT'S IT CALLED? THE DOTS AND DASHES LANGUAGE…"

"Morse code!" you yell. But of course he doesn't understand you.

"HUH…"

Come on!

"OH I BET I CAN LOOK THAT UP TOO. GIVE ME A SECOND."

His character stops moving, it just stares straight at you. You look around a bit, this would be the worst moment for another mob to find you. The player just keeps staring straight.

And that's when you hear T-Bone calling out from the trees. "Rotney! You over here?! Can I help?"

You don't think he can see you yet. What are you going to do?

If you want to call out to him, *turn to page 93*.

If you want to stay silent, *turn to page 88*.

You nod your head. Looking up and down. Up and down.

"YOU'RE NOT EVEN ATTACKING ME. WHAT ARE YOU? AND YOU CAN NOD? THIS IS SERIOUSLY WEIRD. IT'S ALMOST LIKE YOU'RE ANOTHER PLAYER-"

"WAIT"

What's he doing?

"CAN YOU PLEASE JUST NOT EAT ME FOR A SPLIT SECOND?"

You nod your head.

"THIS IS CRAZY."

The player goes still for a couple minutes and then shakes his head again. It's a long couple minutes.

"OKAY, THIS IS CRAZY BUT THERE IS A STORY ON THIS SERVER OF A PLAYER BEING CAUGHT IN A MOB'S BODY WAY BACK WHEN THIS SERVER STARTED, NEAR THE BEGINNING OF MINECRAFT. IT SEEMS IMPOSSIBLE, BUT…"

Is that true? Maybe that means there's a way out?!

"DO YOU KNOW MORSE CODE?"

Weirdly you do, your grandfather made you learn it on a couple particularly boring summer Sunday afternoons.

You nod.

"GOOD. HOP OUT THE DOTS AND DASHES TO COMMUNICATE WITH ME."

What a great idea!

"I am a player trapped in a zombie's body," you hop out to him.

"THIS IS INSANE!" he says after decoding it.

"Can you help me?" you hop.

"OF COURSE. IT'S NOT TOTALLY CLEAR IN THE STORY HOW THE LAST PLAYER GOT OUT, BUT THEY DID."

This is great news!

"THEY DID HOWEVER SPEAK TO A MOB THAT'S NOT TOO FAR AWAY. MAYBE WE START THERE?"

You nod heartily. What other options do you have?

"OKAY, FOLLOW ME."

You head off into the night, along the river, before turning into the mountains. The sun is starting to come up and you guys shelter in a cave for the day. You have to remind the player that you won't survive wandering out and about in the sun like him. You wait patiently together before continuing.

When night comes again, you head out of the cave and back down the mountains, you come into a plain that is full of swamps and small pools, the player leads you right into the middle of it.

Finally, you ask, "Where are we going?"

"I DON'T HAVE TIME TO DECODE YOUR HOPS, BUT DON'T WORRY, WE'RE CLOSE."

You look up to find yourselves in the middle of a village. The village itself is abandoned, there's not a villager in sight. The buildings seem to be a bit run down, a couple vines grow over the walls. A hole here and there suggests that this village has seen some fighting. Something powerful has been here. Maybe a whole army of creepers.

You look at the player who seems to be staring at a building in the center of the town square. You look too, but its hard to make out in the darkness, even with your stellar night vision. You look closer, trying to figure out why she's staring. Then the building moves.

Except it's no building at all. You recognize the huge shoulders, the grey skin and the wandering veins. An Iron Golem pivots in the center of the square to look at you. He stares straight into you. Then charges!

The player throws himself in the way. "NO! STOP! WE NEED YOUR HELP, ELDER GOLEM!"

The Iron Golem stops its lumbering just short of the player. It has the voice of two stones rumbling together and it speaks slowly. "You know your kind is not welcome here, zombie. I am tasked to protect this place."

The player doesn't understand any of this. "WHAT'S HE SAYING?."

Now you don't have time to hop anything out, instead you say, "I am not my kind, Elder Golem. I am a player.

The golem stares.

"WHAT'S HAPPENING?" the player says.

"I may be old, but I'm not foolish, green one. You are a zombie."

"My body may be a zombie, but my mind is a player. I am trapped here, Elder Golem."

There is long, stony, silence. Ha ha, stony. Get it?

Finally, the golem speaks, "Another one? This is a great moment."

"A great moment?" you ask, angrily, "I am trapped here!"

The player shuffles around, "IS HE GOING TO HELP? I HOPE HE CAN HELP, FRIEND."

The golem looks at you. Straight through you. "Welcome Chosen One. We will send you home."

THE END

To find out what happens next, follow your adventure in: Minecraft Zombie Adventure 2: Journey to the Ender.

Congratulations, you made it through to the end of the story! But there are other paths, some less successful, some more, and there are other ways to get to the sequel. Can you find them?

If you want to find out more about me and the other books I've written, flip to the back of the book.

Thanks for reading,

John Diary

"No, I don't want to go," you say.

"Don't be stupid. Don't be a zombie, Rotney."

"I'm not being stupid! I like you. There's something about you too. That's why I want to stick around."

She looks at you happily, there's a flash in those pixely black eyes.

"Really, that's what you want?" she asks.

"Yes!" you say. "I mean, I also want to find out why I'm stuck like this. And I kind of want to go home, to my family, and to my world, where I don't have a taste for brains. But if I'm going to be here, I want you to be around. I hope that don't sound mean."

"No, of course not!" She thinks for a second. "I totally understand wanting to go home. Of course you want to go home."

She thinks for another second.

"I might be... able to help?"

"What?" you say, really acting the part of a dumb zombie now. Good work!

"There's a story," she says, "a story that my mommy creeper used to tell me on some long days to pass the time. It's an old mob story, about a player who became a mob. A skeleton, in this case."

You're distracted by the thought of a mommy creeper. Do creepers have babies? How does that work? You don't want to think about it. Stay focused now, what she's saying could be important!

"Maybe it's nothing, but if it was true, well- In that story he found a way to get out of the skeleton and change back into a player. So maybe the same could happen to you."

"Really, you think it might have happened before?"

"Maybe."

"Well, how did the player in the story get back?"

"I don't remember, that wasn't the part of the story that anyone really pays attention to, it seemed silly, frankly," she says.

"It does," you agree.

"But, I know someone who would know, come on."

You help Teagan down the ladder. It's a bit terrifying, she's not comfortable with it, but you find staying close and talking her through it helps a lot and soon you're on the ground.

You head off into the night, along the river, before turning into the mountains. The sun is starting to come up and you guys shelter in a cave for the day. You have to remind Teagan that you won't survive wandering out and about in the sun like her. She waits patiently with you and you try to tell her about the outside world, she listens with rapt attention.

When night comes again, you head out of the cave and back down the mountains, you come into a plain that is full of swamps and small pools, Teagan leads you right into the middle of it.

Finally, you ask, "Where are we going Teagan?"

"To see the only mob in this world that will know how to help you."

"Why? Who are they?"

"A creature some say is as old as the world itself."

You look up to find yourselves in the middle of a village. The village itself is abandoned, there's not a villager in sight. The buildings seem to be a bit run down, a couple vines grow over the walls. A hole here and there suggests that this village has seen some fighting. Something powerful has been here. Maybe a whole army of creepers.

You look at Teagan who seems to be staring at a building in the center of the town square. You look too, but its hard to make out in the darkness, even with your stellar night vision. You look closer, trying to figure out why she's staring. Then the building moves.

Except it's no building at all. You recognize the huge shoulders, the grey skin and the wandering veins. An Iron Golem pivots in the center of the square to look at you. He stares straight into you. Then charges!

Teagan throws herself in the way. "No! Stop! He's with me!"

The Iron Golem stops its lumbering just short of Teagan. It has the voice of two stones rumbling together and it speaks slowly. "You know his kind is not welcome here. I keep this place safe."

Teagan seems to not be intimidated by its huge size. "That's the thing, he isn't his kind."

The golem stares.

"He isn't a zombie." Teagan says.

"I may be old, but I'm not foolish, explosive one. This is a zombie."

"His body may be a zombie, but his mind is a player. He is a player, Elder Golem."

There is long, stony, silence. Ha ha, stony. Get it?

Finally, the golem speaks, "Another one? You know what this means, explosive one. Don't you?"

Teagan nods.

Then the golem looks at you. Straight through you. "Welcome Chosen One. We will send you home."

THE END.

To find out what happens next, follow your adventure in: Minecraft Zombie Adventure 2: Journey to the Ender.

John Diary

Congratulations, you made it through to the end of the story! But there are other paths, some less successful, some more, and there are other ways to get to the sequel. Can you find them?

If you want to find out more about me and the other books I've written, flip to the back of the book.

Thanks for reading,

John Diary

You head off into the night, along the river, before turning into the mountains. The sun is starting to come up and you guys shelter in a cave for the day. You have to remind the player that you won't survive wandering out and about in the sun like him. You wait patiently together before continuing.

When night comes again, you head out of the cave and back down the mountains, you come into a plain that is full of swamps and small pools, the player leads you right into the middle of it.

Finally, you ask, "Where are we going?"

"I DON'T HAVE TIME TO DECODE YOUR HOPS, BUT DON'T WORRY, WE'RE CLOSE."

You look up to find yourselves in the middle of a village. The village itself is abandoned, there's not a villager in sight. The buildings seem to be a bit run down, a couple vines grow over the walls. A hole here and there suggests that this village has seen some fighting. Something powerful has been here. Maybe a whole army of creepers.

You look at the player who seems to be staring at a building in the center of the town square. You look too, but its hard to make out in the darkness, even with your stellar night vision. You look closer, trying to figure out why she's staring. Then the building moves.

Except it's no building at all. You recognize the huge shoulders, the grey skin and the wandering veins. An Iron Golem pivots in the center of the square to look at you. He stares straight into you. Then charges!

The player throws himself in the way. "NO! STOP! WE NEED YOUR HELP, ELDER GOLEM!"

The Iron Golem stops its lumbering just short of the player. It has the voice of two stones rumbling together and it speaks slowly. "You know your kind is not welcome here, zombie. I am tasked to protect this place."

The player doesn't understand any of this. "WHAT'S HE SAYING?."

Now you don't have time to hop anything out, instead you say, "I am not my kind, Elder Golem. I am a player.

The golem stares.

"WHAT'S HAPPENING?" the player says.

"I may be old, but I'm not foolish, green one. You are a zombie."

"My body may be a zombie, but my mind is a player. I am trapped here, Elder Golem."

There is long, stony, silence. Ha ha, stony. Get it?

Finally, the golem speaks, "Another one? This is a great moment."

"A great moment?" you ask, angrily, "I am trapped here!"

The player shuffles around, "IS NO ONE GOING TO TELL ME WHAT'S HAPPENING?! MOBS ARE THE WORST."

The golem looks at you. Straight through you. "Welcome Chosen One. We will send you home."

THE END

To find out what happens next, follow your adventure in: Minecraft Zombie Adventure 2: Journey to the Ender.

Congratulations, you made it through to the end of the story! But there are other paths, some less successful, some more, and there are other ways to get to the sequel. Can you find them?

If you want to find out more about me and the other books I've written, check out the next couple pages.

- John Diary

The Sequel

Find out what happens next in the sequel: The Zombie Adventure 2. Find out what the golem means by *'Chosen One'!* Go on countless adventures: solve a labyrinth, build a portal, deal with some annoying, french silverfish, outsmart a posse full of self-obsessed endermen, and make friends with a strange old villager.

Can *you* find your way home?

Other Books by John Diary

Another Minecraft Choose Your Own Story! You'll love this!

From best-selling children's author, John Diary, comes the heart-warming and gut-busting tale of Sneezy Steve. He has just spawned in the world of Minecraft with nothing: no memories, no items and no clue what to do next. The only thing he does have is a mysterious photograph in the bottom of his backpack.

What happens next? I can't even tell you, because in this Choose Your Own Story book, YOU are the author, you get to decide what happens to poor little Steve. Will he befriend a block of dirt? Or make an army of zombies? Or just pretend that he's a wolf all day? It's up to you!

Love Choose Your Own Story? Want to be a wizard? This book's for you.

You receive a mysterious invitation to a magical school where you can learn the secrets of wizardry and magic. Take an air ship ride to the castle, get sorted into a house based on the decisions that you make, compete in wizarding sports and fight against an evil plot that is making the students in the school do some very strange things…

If you've always wanted to go to a wizarding school, there's finally a book that can take you there.

The Minecraft adventure that you've been waiting for!

Dan is playing Minecraft with his friends, like he always does, when a strange figure, white from head-to-toe, approaches him in the game and drops a book at his feet. Cautiously, Dan reads the book: it's an invitation, to a school. A school for only the very best Minecraft players in the country.

What follows is an exciting adventure full of spying, intrigue, saving the world, and of course all the normal middle school stuff too.

Hi Reader,

Thanks so much for reading! I hope you really enjoyed this book!

Would you do me a favour? It's tough getting started as a new author. Even if your book is really good, there are hundreds of books online and people might not be able to find yours. But you can help me with this. **If you leave a review on my book, it will help other people find it, and will let me know that you want me to write more!**

It doesn't have to be a long review or well-written. Just search for Minecraft Zombie Adventure on Amazon and find the book. Scroll down. Click on 'Write a Customer Review', click on the stars and write a couple words. It would mean so much to me! Thank you!

If you want to find out more about me and my books you can go to **johndiary.com.**

If you want to read more Choose Your Own Stories, you can get a free Choose Your Own Story book when you join my fan club at johndiary.com/signup. Just put in your e-mail address and I'll send you a book for free. Also I'll send you free previews of my books when they come out! And get the chance to win future books! It's pretty exciting in the fan club. Join now!

You can also keep up with me online:

Facebook: John Diary at facebook.com/johndiarybooks

Twitter: @johndiarybooks

Instagram: johndiarybooks

Keep reading! Keep choosing!

You're the best,

John Diary

48418577R00073

Made in the USA
Lexington, KY
16 August 2019